CU00920978

This fascinating collection of essays is about physically and psychically encountering the environment, mainly through walking. The focus is on the impact on our interior experience of moving mindfully through exterior space. The authors demonstrate, by means of personal and often poetic narrative, how built and open spaces contribute to mood, emotion, behaviour – even to the construction of our personalities. Some emphasise how organised space helps or hinders their personal growth and enlightenment. Others focus on the urban environment's relation to gender, race, power relations and the arts. This is psychogeography in action, with ideas that are rooted in the European Situationist movement. These carefully edited chapters offer a rich read that will expand the clinical horizons of our profession.

**Wyn Bramley, psychotherapist, trainer, couple therapist, group analyst and author. Her latest book is *The Mature Psychotherapist: beyond training and ideology***

This lively collection of essays brings together for the very first time two unmistakably connected fields. The contributors' subjective accounts – which is what psychogeography is about, after all – neatly suture geographical responses to the inner life of individuals. Some use walking as a form of psychotherapeutic practice and here demonstrate how the act of walking can bring about affective change, enabling people to modify their inner life through direct engagement with the outer world. The collection also includes many beautiful illustrations from a number of artists.

**Dr Tina Richardson, cultural theorist and psychogeographer, Manchester Metropolitan University**

This book brings together the growing international imperative to creatively engage with and articulate the complexities of psychogeographical experience and the expanding field of more activist, place-oriented social psychotherapy. Each of its 10 chapters is grounded in particular stories, bodies and places, thereby carefully placing these general concerns through specific explorations of affects, micro-politics, troubles, urban vernaculars and distinctive senses of mapping and play. Consequently, the book makes a valuable contribution in helping us to register, and hopefully maintain and cherish, a much greater number of alternative ways of belonging to the world.

**Dr Iain Biggs, independent lecturer/artist/researcher, honorary research fellow at the University of Dundee and visiting research fellow at Bath Spa University**

# Psychogeography and Psychotherapy:

## CONNECTING PATHWAYS

Edited by

CHRIS ROSE

First published 2019

PCCS Books Ltd
Wyastone Business Park
Wyastone Leys
Monmouth
NP25 3SR
UK

Tel +44 (0)1600 891509
contact@pccs-books.co.uk
www.pccs-books.co.uk

This collection © Chris Rose, 2019
The individual chapters © the contributors, 2019
Illustrations © the artists, 2019

All rights reserved.
No part of this publication may be reproduced, stored in a retrieval system, trans-
mitted or utilised in any form by any means, electronic, mechanical, photocopying
or recording or otherwise, without permission in writing from the publishers.

The authors have asserted their right to be identified as the authors
of this work in accordance with the Copyright, Designs and Patents Act 1988.

*Psychogeography and Psychotherapy: connecting pathways*

British Library Cataloguing in Publication Data.
A catalogue record for this book is available from the British Library

ISBN 978 1 910919 47 7

Cover design by Jason Anscomb
Cover illustration by Simone Ridyard
Printed in the UK by Short Run Press, Exeter

# Psychogeography and Psychotherapy: connecting pathways

## Contents

## Illustrations

## Acknowledgements

With thanks to all the contributors for their creativity and hard work, and for being such a resourceful and helpful group. Thanks are also due to others whose work doesn't appear here but who have made a valuable contribution behind the scenes: Alex Bridger, Myira Khan, Helen George, Jason Hughes, Annie Shaw, and Isabel Carmona. Particular thanks go to Catherine Jackson and colleagues at PCCS Books.

## Dedication

To Louis and the Ancestors

# Preface

The book in your hands is the product of the efforts and creativity of many people, but where does it come from? Psychodynamic psychotherapies have always been asking that question, intrigued by the many ways in which the past cannot be separated from the present. 'Where', of course, is a word denoting place, but we have traditionally been more interested in 'when', bypassing the burgeoning academic interest in place. It was only when a number of things came together in my own life that I began to appreciate its significance and richness.

Becoming involved in urban sketching had the effect of drawing my attention to the built environment, its beauty and its ugliness – seeing how much was shaped by commerce, cars, shopping, warehousing, and how little by people and community. Then co-presenting an art exhibition on 'Home' and moving house together triggered an ongoing exploration into the nature of belonging in a particular geographical environment. I became interested in the idea that we could have a very early relationship with our physical, geographic environment that could resonate in various circumstances throughout life – rather in the way that our earliest linguistic patterns can be brought to life many years later with an appropriate trigger.

Into this mix came *Walking Inside Out* (Richardson, 2015), with its inspiring, witty, provocative contributions that convinced me that psychotherapy and psychogeography had some very interesting things to talk over with each other. My hope is that this book will inspire more walks and conversations, as we open ourselves to learn from each other.

*Chris Rose*

## Reference

Richardson T (ed) (2015). *Walking Inside Out: contemporary British psychogeography*. London: Rowman and Littlefield.

# Introduction
## Chris Rose

Pathways that connect together open up fresh possibilities of exploration. They can create new and varied routes, where psychotherapy and psychogeography may walk together, each encouraging the other to take the next step. It's a walk that may be companionable – sharing an appreciation of the surroundings, discussing subjects of mutual interest; argumentative – one in front of the other, a long way apart or squeezed together on a narrow pathway; playful or earnest – inventing or recalling stories about the location; thoughtful, provocative – bouncing ideas from one to the other.

These are my hopes for this book, for it seems to me that psychotherapy and psychogeography have a mutually enriching relationship – one that has not been widely acknowledged but can open productive, new areas for theoretical, experiential and professional exploration. As the two of them walk together through the different chapters here, they bring the possibility of a wider and richer vision for all concerned.

As a psychotherapist, I know a lot more about one partner in the walk than the other. However, as is always the case, as we get to know someone, we realise that the labels we use are too limiting and inadequate to capture the reality. Psychotherapists and psychogeographers might seem very distinct categories from a distance, but each label incorporates an enormous variety of people, practices and ideas.

Psychogeography sprawls across many traditional academic demarcations and, like psychotherapy, is a model of multidisciplinary cross-fertilisation. This makes a concise definition difficult, and that flexibility is perhaps one of its strengths. There are many varieties and definitions of psychogeographies (eg. Richardson, 2015), but here I want to introduce psychogeography via those pathways that first attracted me, in the hope that, along the myriad routes, there will be something that resonates with each reader.

There seems to me to be two key elements to the definition. Psychogeography is concerned with the effect of geographical location on emotion and behaviour; this is tied to an emphasis on walking, paying critical attention to the (generally but not exclusively) urban landscape and the power structures that have shaped it. There has been much written about the impact of the 'natural environment' and its part in therapy, so the bias towards urban living provides a helpful balance, while acknowledging that the boundary between 'natural/rural' and 'man-made/urban' is by no means straightforward.

Psychogeography pays attention to the shaping power of the environmental context on human existence, and it is this awareness of context that is shared with psychotherapy, particularly systemic and group versions. Group psychotherapy, for example, pays sustained and concentrated attention to the power of the relational environment that both clients and therapists inhabit and make. It is the context of others that shapes who we are and who we in turn shape. In groups, especially long-term ones, we witness the process whereby members insistently draw out and co-create their familiar relational environment until, we hope, they are liberated by a growing capacity to understand and challenge these replays of ingrained patterns.

Any account of being human that reduces an individual to a singleton in a world of singletons is missing the point. We are who we are in the context of others, and this is itself situated in a physical, environmental context. Our relational experiences are the raw material from which our selves are constructed, and so too are our experiences of the wider environment. This systemic thinking forms the major highway between psychogeography and psychotherapy. Identity is tied to place. The environment is not the backdrop; it is woven through our identity.

Who we are and where we feel at home are bound together. The word 'home' itself conjures geographical location, emotional resonances, attachments, images, memories and more. It straddles the external and internal landscape in a way that demonstrates the permeable boundary between the two. We each, according to Fitzgerald and Rose (2015), inhabit:

> ... not an 'objective' space, but our own cognitive map of place and space, freighted with affects and memories, with its risks and hazards, its threats and lures, its familiarities and alien places, its locales of sanctity, solidarity, support, and much more.

We find ourselves attracted not only to particular people but to places too; like a fingerprint, we have a unique patterned response to our environment created through our experience. Certain landscapes, streets, atmospheres, colours, sights, sounds and smells resonate and can teach us much about our own selves, if we pay attention. Spatial metaphors abound in the psychotherapeutic vernacular. A safe space, where you're at, stuck in a corner, deep in a hole, falling through space – we so often turn to geography to find words for our experiences, so we should not be surprised that the geographical environment shapes our identity. Exploring our own relationship to place can be a rewarding pathway to personal development.

Therapists working with older people, and especially those with dementia, will recognise the way in which places remain embedded in even the most fragmented of memories. Andrea Capstick (2015), using walking interviews, finds that communication thought to be meaningless can accurately reference particular places in the past. She challenges the act of locating 'amnesia' solely in the individual when it is as much to do with living in a society that undervalues and forgets its own past.

> The destruction of memory lies as much in the outer world with its demolition sites, road widening schemes, bomb damage, slum clearance and gentrification as it does in the 'damaged' brain of the person with dementia. (Capstick, 2015: 212)

Here again is that systemic understanding that locates *who* we are amidst *where* and *when* we are and were. This interconnectedness plays out in the therapy room too. *What* is said is linked to *where* it is said; to disclose our most intimate feelings we need a sense of emotional and physical security that derives in part from the place we are in. In our own therapy rooms, we may attempt to create spaces that are containing but not intrusive, calm but not cosy, interesting but not over stimulating. However, most of us have also worked in spaces that we have no control over, that are hostile to the task in hand: rooms full of desks, cupboard-sized spaces, consulting rooms with hospital beds and screens, rooms with stained carpets, off noisy corridors, and so on. Neither patients, clients, students nor therapists can fail to be aware of the powerful intrusions from the physical environment. Once we begin to explore this, along with the possible resonance with previous environments, we will probably be led into a consideration of power: who controls this space, who decides its usage, and who is excluded from the decision-making, for example. This way it becomes even clearer that it is not only who we are that is profoundly shaped by place, but that place involves power.

Psychogeography brings our attention to the ways in which the spaces we move through and inhabit are controlled by particular interests. Gated communities, CCTV cameras, car-dominated routes, huge parking areas, gentrification, regeneration, lighting, signage, street furniture, graffiti, litter; places where men may walk but women avoid; no-go zones and threatening streets. The more we question the ways in which our environments are designed, built and used, the more we become aware of the values and interests that are shaping the terrain. Thinking about this on an everyday walk in our own areas may be an eye-opening exercise.

> Looking around at our streets, it's startling when you first notice it: like waking from a dream and forgetting where you are.
> A moment of disorientation as your eyes make sense of the shadows and see the room for what it is.
> After that, it's unmistakable: our streets are not our own.
> From the parked cars that line the roads to the traffic that speeds

along them, in many of our cities we are second-class citizens if we're not inside a motor vehicle. (Laker, 2016)

This is one reason why psychogeographers walk rather than drive. Walking can bring us into contact with the environment in a visceral and attentive way. Walking allows time to look closely, to think and to explore. Walking in a psychogeographical sense is not the same as a stroll or ramble: it is observant, analytic and self-reflective. Psychogeographers find unfamiliar routes; individually or as part of a group, they wander without preconceived ideas of destination and record the subjective experience in a multitude of styles. The kinaesthetic qualities of movement combine with reflection and analysis in a way that can disrupt our habitual responses and open us to new appreciations and energies.

Whether we walk or not, we psychotherapists and counsellors recognise its potential. As therapy, or part of therapy, it is used in many different formats: in groups or alone, with mindfulness, with or without therapists, in conjunction with other interventions or on its own. Walking appears to have an effect that is unrelated to energy expenditure or exercise *per se*, and is often recommended as a component in the treatment for depression (Robertson et al, 2012).

There is a substantial body of research looking at the impact of space on mental health. Laura McGrath (2012) examines the impact of different types of space on people with mental illness, and argues that experiences of distress, rather than being determined by static internal processes, are contextualised. Those deemed to be 'mad', who once would have been in the designated space of an asylum, are now 'in the community'. A similar redesignation of space has happened with looked-after children and those with special needs and disabilities. Losing the allocated space of the asylum, special school or children's home and becoming part of the 'community' creates a context that often belies the warm connotations of the phrase. For many, the reality is surveillance rather than support, and some find themselves literally excluded to the least attractive margins of available public space – rough sleeping in derelict areas, underpasses and pavements.

Osborne (2015) writes about the milieu – the space we live in, 'cut from' the environment material available. Cities, he suggests, are overlapping series of diverse and contradictory milieus:

> … milieus for some and not others, milieus for the rich, milieus for certain kind of business enterprise, milieus for consumption, and so on but not a single milieu of any sort. And for the excluded and dispossessed, cities are indeed simply environments.

It seems to me that therapy cannot afford to ignore issues of space any more than it can ignore social justice. Psychogeography offers a radical, subversive, challenging critique of space that psychotherapy can benefit from.

In addition, it offers fun. Winnicott would certainly have applauded the playfulness and creativity that psychogeography embraces. Walks may be directed by rolling a dice, for example, or following the gaze of a CCTV camera. Such walks are arbitrary, whimsical, free associative wanderings that allow unconscious processes the space to flourish. Critical psychologist Alex Bridger (2015) uses walking-based research methodologies derived from psychogeographical ideas, arguing that their playfulness can challenge routine behaviour and assumptions and promote creative rethinking about urban space. Psychogeography challenges the dominance of the cognitive in understanding the world, pushes against boundaries and conventions, honours the subjective experience – surely enough common ground to establish a mutually enriching relationship with psychotherapy?

These themes are woven through the chapters in this book, whether in the foreground or background. It is impossible to neatly group the chapters or impose a logical sequence on them. All of the authors write from and about personal experiences, so the chapters form a kind of group conversation. Themes are picked up and then interrupted, only to reappear later, intensified, clarified and challenged in the rich swirl of resonances.

Diane Parker is a dance movement therapist and brings a focused bodily awareness to her considerations of the interplay between therapy and psychogeography. Her chapter, 'Outside in, inside out', is a personal reflection on her work with two groups of people with complex mental health problems: one in a secure hospital setting and the other in a community centre. She explores the impact of the physical environment on herself as a female therapist, and on her client group, paying particular attention to somatic and gendered responses. She writes of the ways in which the women in her single-sex groups inhabit their bodies and the environment, and how this translates through creative movement and verbal expression.

Jane Samuels, in 'Taking space', argues that it is possible to create a personal relationship with the city, despite its alienating and sometimes hostile face. By 'taking space' in this way, there is a reciprocating sense of containment whereby the city 'holds space' for the individual. This is not a romanticised view of city life, as her description of the 2017 bombing at the Manchester Arena and her own personal narrative both demonstrate. However, she sees that forging relationships with places fosters a sense of belonging that can support self-actualisation, in the Rogerian sense.

'Room to breathe', the title of Chris Powell's chapter, is also the name of a walking project he organises for people working in mental health. Here the archetypical lone, male walker of classic psychogeography joins up with others, and the classic analytic group picks up its chairs and heads outside. The physical wandering, or *dérive*, is aligned with the process of free association, as a sort of internal *dérive* – a connection that will appear in various chapters throughout the book. This group has its basis in applied group analysis, but meets four times a year, at different seasons, to walk in the Yorkshire Dales, where the presence of others deepens and amplifies the gains of both walking and being outside. A special group meeting was convened for the purposes of this chapter, and here Chris captures the participants' reflections on the emotions, sensations and thoughts generated by this experience.

Benedict Hoff and Richard Phillips are engaged in another piece of action research, as reported in their chapter, 'Mindfulness in the city'. Growing out of Richard's research into curiosity and 'taking notice' – one of five ways to mental wellbeing endorsed by the government – they looked at the benefits of mindfulness in an urban environment. Participants in three workshops held in different parts of London were given some formal practice in meditation to develop the necessary skills of 'taking notice' before walking in the city. The outcomes point not only to a greater sensory attunement but also to an increased tolerance of the challenging aspects of the environment, suggesting that therapeutic landscapes are not necessarily located in attractive rural places but are a function of the ways in which we relate to them.

Liz Bondi writes from her experience as both an academic in human geography and a practising psychotherapist. In 'Feeling my way', she describes how her body-in-space reacts before, during and after a psychotherapy session. She explores the subjective use of her walk to and from the session, as well as the micro-geographies of the setting itself, and connects these to the internal landscapes experienced in the encounter with the client. She describes an intrapersonal and interpersonal relational web that flickers with glimpses and senses of place triggered by physical location and its memories.

In 'Moving, loitering and resisting', Morag Rose talks with me about the psychogeographical walking group she and others have established in Manchester. The Loiterers Resistance Movement is a fluid, assorted group that meets once a month to thoughtfully and peacefully wander through the streets, taking notice, and in so doing challenges the encroaching privatisation and commercialisation of the city. Intended as both fun and a prompt for critical analysis of the environment, with its overt and hidden agendas, these walks have attracted many people since they began in 2006. Morag explains their origins, influences and practices and her determination that the streets should be for everyone.

Phil Wood, in 'The theory and practice of urban therapy', challenges us to think of places as organic and sentient, capable of being hurt and damaged. Therapeutic planning connects urban policy and psychological wellbeing and requires a holistic approach untrammelled by professional or cultural demarcations. The introductory discussion of relevant theory leads into his personal experiences of working in the cities of Birmingham and Huddersfield, and takes us out of the UK into Rotterdam, Mostar and Lisbon.

Karen Izod also deliberates on the multi-faceted relationship between place – *here* – and identity – *who I am* – while inviting the reader to tune into their own reactions and resonances as they read the piece. Her chapter, 'Here is where I have a presence', is a poetic, associative drift that finds itself in complex themes of place, attachment, loss and change. She writes about the unconscious transference of meanings from one place and time to another, and how the sensory experience of place is bound together with our earliest relationship with caregivers. It is a piece of writing that needs digesting over time, like the poetry it contains.

There are strong resonances here with Valentina Krajnović, who is also thinking about the impact of place on identity. For her, the breakup of Yugoslavia meant losing both a home and a country, and she describes how she tried to build a new home in London while violence was tearing apart her former one. Walking through the city, she finds places that have particular significance, noticing the recurrence of the uncanny, the indistinct and the in-between. She links a powerful personal narrative with ideas from group analysis, including those relating to large groups.

Having mapped out, albeit briefly, the territory of the book, I want to consider the map itself. It seems that map-making is an activity that is wired into humanity. Carved about 4,000 years ago, the Bedolina petroglyph at Valcamonica in Italy is one of the oldest known maps in existence (Harmon, 2004). We constantly map what is around us – the terrain, routes, geology, seas, space – and what is within us – magnetic resonance imagery being the contemporary 'scientific' version of that. Maps are our attempts to orient ourselves in an environment and to grasp not only where we are but who we are.

> We all travel with many maps, neatly folded and tucked away in the glove compartment of memory – some of them communal and universal, like our autonomic familiarity with seasonal constellations and the shape of continents, and some as particular as the local roads that we have all traipsed. (Hall, in Harmon, 2004: 15)

Psychotherapy has a close association with maps. As we 'walk alongside' the client, we travel through internal landscapes of desired utopias and feared hells in order to find new pathways through old and scarred territory. We examine and unearth buried cities and civilisations, patiently expose skeletons and artefacts, draw up timelines and map future projects. In my own experience, geography, geology, archaeology and cartography all meet in psychotherapy, and this shapes my concluding chapter, 'Mapmaking'.

Throughout the book, the chapters are punctuated by sketches of different locations in different styles. These images of urban environments are not illustrations of the words but free-standing statements. The artists are all part of the community of 'urban sketchers' who draw on location, individually and in groups, recording people and places throughout the world.[1] Like psychogeographers, they pay close attention to the urban environment, challenging our habitual visual snapshots of familiar sights and helping us to see in new ways.

So that is the book, and I hope that within it you will find riches and resonances. Of course, it has its limitations. This book presents a white, European perspective that is limited in its cultural and racial diversity, thereby inadvertently reflecting the history of both psychogeography and psychotherapy. There will be another book, I sincerely hope, that will break free from these limitations. This one is an imperfect and incomplete introduction to what I hope will become a far more diverse and creative exploration of the powerful bond between people and place.

As psychotherapists and counsellors, we recognise the ongoing struggle to relate at depth to the other; in our thinking too, we need to cross boundaries. Engaging with other disciplines is part of the process of expanding our cross-cultural communicative possibilities and understandings. Encountering psychogeography is like greeting an old friend and simultaneously discovering a stimulating, quirky, innovative and challenging new acquaintance. As Stephen Hall (2004: 18) writes:

> (T)he most important thing a map shows, if we pause to look at it long enough, if we travel upon it widely enough, if we think about it hard enough, is all the things we still do not know.

---

1. www.urbansketchers.org

## References

Bondi L (2005). *Making Connections and Thinking Through Emotions: between geography and psychotherapy.* Edinburgh: Institute of Geography, University of Edinburgh.

Bridger AJ (2015). Psychogeography, antipsychologies and the question of social change. In: Richardson T (ed). *Walking Inside Out: contemporary British psychogeography.* London: Rowman & Littlefield (pp227–240).

Capstick A (2015). Rewalking the city: people with dementia. In: Richardson T (ed). *Walking Inside Out: contemporary British psychogeography.* London: Rowman & Littlefield (pp221-226).

Fitzgerald D, Rose N (2015). *The neurosocial city.* [Blog.] Urban Transformations. www.urbantransformations.ox.ac.uk/debate/the-neurosocial-city (accessed 25 March 2019).

Hall S (2004). I, Mercator. In: Harmon K. *You Are Here: personal geographies and other maps of the imagination.* New York, NY: Princeton Architectural Press (pp15–35).

Harmon K (2004). *You Are Here: personal geographies and other maps of the imagination.* New York, NY: Princeton Architectural Press.

Laker L (2016). Will car drivers ever learn to share the road with bikes? *The Guardian*; 28 September. www.theguardian.com/cities/2016/sep/28 (accessed 25 March 2019).

McGrath L (2012). *Heterotopias of Mental Health Care: the role of space in experiences of distress, madness, and mental health service use.* PhD thesis. London: University of East London. www.researchgate.net/publication/263964602

Osborne T (2015). *Should we look to develop a renewed vitalism of the city?* Comment. [Online.] Urban Transformations. www.urbantransformations.ox.ac.uk/debate/the-neurosocial-city/should-we-look-to-develop-a-renewed-vitalism-of-the-city (accessed 25 March 2019).

Richardson T (ed) (2015). *Walking Inside Out: contemporary British psychogeography.* London: Rowman and Littlefield.

Robertson R, Robertson A, Jepson R, Maxwell M (2012). Walking for depression or depressive symptoms: a systematic review and meta-analysis. *Mental Health and Physical Activity* 5(1): 66–75.

# 1 | Outside in and inside out: an embodied and gendered response to space and place

## Diane Parker

Dance movement psychotherapists use movement analysis as a lens through which to see and enhance our understanding of our clients. We study the way in which someone moves in relationship to others and their external environment, using creative movement as a form of expression, and then use this to inform our relationships with our clients as we create a 'dancing dialogue' together, either one-to-one or in a group context. The first and most direct experience of movement analysis begins with the self, through observation and awareness of our own habitual patterns, rhythms and shapes – our use of weight, space and time – and, crucially, how and when these change in relationship to other and the environment (Koch & Bender, 2007).

For me, nowhere is this more evident than in basic walking. A life-long city dweller, I have never owned a car and rely on public transport and my own feet to get me from A to B. My dance therapy training and introduction to movement analysis gave me a language with which to understand how a simple walk can be influenced by the environment and circumstances. My Sunday afternoon wander through the local park looks and feels very different to the walk I make through an unfamiliar part of town at night. Free, loose, light and open becomes tight, heavy, rapid and closed. The extension of my limbs from the core of my body becomes tighter and smaller as my kinesphere (Laban, 1966) (the imaginary space around my body, whose periphery can be reached by extended limbs) shrinks considerably – an automatic fear response.

As a woman, I also notice the automatic changes in tension in my body as I move through the city – moments when I become more alert and aware, sensing potential danger, whether justified or not. Tall buildings, sightlines obscured by sharp corners, darkened areas or areas hidden from public view, such as underpasses, all signify a need for increased alertness and awareness. Similarly, public spaces with a dominant male presence, where men gather as a tribe and make vocal, public displays of aggression – pubs, clubs, construction sites and football grounds – can be intimidating, and I note how my body and my movement pattern respond accordingly. The shift in muscular tension reflects a change in felt sense, as my internal landscape changes in response to my perception of my external landscape. My body responds intuitively to this new environment and my relationship to it: do I *belong* here? Am I *at home* here? Am I *safe*? The gendered body has a wisdom and a language of its own.

The relationship between body and gender is ever complex and intense. In rejecting the essentialist conviction that physicality determines gender, we do not separate gender from the body, for if gender is something that we *do* rather than what we *are*, then the body has a central role in the performance. We read gender from gait, the set of the shoulders, seating positions, gestures etc, and we learn unconsciously what body movements and styles are considered appropriate for our own gender. When the man sitting next to us takes us all the space, with his legs set apart, he is performing masculinity – a practice so established that it might be seen as 'natural', rather than as a statement of gender and power. My own bodily responses and movements are constructed in this binary gendered environment – one that, despite some encouraging signs of relaxation, still dominates our culture.

It is late spring, and the morning air is fragrant with blossom, petrol fumes and possibility. In this leafy enclave of south London, the morning commute is well underway, and I am walking the route I take twice a week to the psychiatric hospital where I work on clinical placement as a trainee dance movement psychotherapist. A ten-minute walk along the main road up from the station, a sharp right turn, and suddenly the traffic noise falls away, receding into the distance as I approach the driveway of the old Victorian hospital, standing in its beautiful gardens. The trees are bursting with colour today, abundant with pink and white blossoms, some of which are starting to fall, peppering the grass like so much wedding confetti. My body feels loose, light and open, warmed and supple from my brisk walk up from the station and the morning sun on my skin. My internal landscape matches that of the environment – I feel a sense of something budding, coming to fruition, of possibilities and potential. I am nearing the end of my placement and my training, and my future lies ahead of me like a golden ribbon of opportunity. There is some uncertainty about what this day, this month, this season will bring, but I feel a sense of grounded curiosity as my feet carry me into the hospital and towards the office where I and my fellow arts therapists are based.

Some time later, I leave the office and walk across the hospital grounds to the forensic clinic where my clients are held. This time, as I look up at the pink-and-white trees and unblemished blue sky, I feel a sense of longing and sadness, as though I am capturing this image in an effort to hold onto it for the next couple of hours. As I take this walk towards the clinic, it never fails to strike me that this experience of crossing the grounds and drinking in the beautiful spring landscape is one that my clients rarely share. Specifically, I am aware of the sense of being free, at home in the world, at one with the changing seasons, in alignment with the landscape.

As I enter the clinic, I show my identity pass at the gate and am handed a bunch of heavy keys, which I strap into the leather pouch around my hips. I enter the women's ward, first looking up at the concave mirror above the door that shows the main corridor towards the nurses' office. All clear. Turn the keys twice anti-clockwise, push open the door. Turn back towards the door, turn the keys twice clockwise. Check the door is locked behind me by giving it a firm shake. Now turn to face the nurses' station and walk down the corridor. This procedure has a familiar shape and rhythm to it; the glance at the mirror, the jangle, whirr and click of keys; open, slam, jangle, whirr and click, jiggle and turn.

The assault on the senses – bright fluorescent lights, the clatter and chatter of high-pitched female voices, the sickly aroma of cleaning fluid, perfumed air freshener and lingering smells of toast from the ward kitchen. As I walk down the corridor, my body responds to this new environment accordingly: my movements are muscular and boundaried, my stride strong and heavy, my hips weighed down by the leather pouch holding keys and electronic alarm. My heels strike the floor purposefully and my gaze is fixed directly on the nurses' station ahead of me.

At the time, I was co-facilitating a mixed-sex weekly dance movement psychotherapy group in the clinic, which necessitated collecting clients from both the women's and the men's wards every week. My female co-lead and I would take turns to fetch either the men or the women from the wards and bring them together for the group. I noticed a subtle shift in my responses between the male and female environments, which I explored with my fellow trainees.

Dance movement psychotherapists can also use other creative media in the therapeutic work with our clients – voice, music, words, images and play with props such as fabric and toys. During an experiential creative exercise with other trainees using art materials, I created two contrasting images on paper. The first was awash with shades of sickly yellow and a colour I can only describe as 'puce green'. The second was a headache-inducing noise of violent reds and throbbing purples. Rose (2017) has written about how we ascribe mood to place and how the use of colour and light are instrumental in making this distinction. Discussing this with my peer trainees, I realised I had externalised through art-making my own visceral countertransference response to the wards in the forensic clinic. Somatically, on the men's ward this translated to a sensation of passive collapse, numbness and mild nausea, reflecting the mood of a space populated by patients for whom the most common diagnosis was anti-social personality disorder, who were numb with medication and for whom 'feeling' was experienced as dangerous. By contrast, my somatic response to the women's ward was one of violence and passion and overwhelming need and hunger. Interestingly, my perception of 'danger' was more heightened on the women's ward than in the men's ward, where perhaps the sense of numbness anaesthetised any threat.

Apart from the logistical challenges in terms of dynamic administration and risk management, my co-lead and I were also aware of the emotional impact of bringing together a group of male and female offenders, some of whom had committed violent crimes and/or experienced intimate partner violence and childhood sexual abuse. Though we hoped that a mixed-sex group would give the female members an opportunity to challenge their own perceptions of 'men are abusers, women are abused', the women's bodies told a revealing story.

Caroline, one of the women, referred herself to join the group by reaching out and grabbing my arm as I was walking down the corridor of the women's ward early on in my placement. I noticed at the time that, although the upper part of her body was bound and closed – shoulders narrowed and rounded, arms tightly held against her torso – the lower half was expansive and open – she sat on the floor with her legs splayed widely apart. As she was a heavily obese woman, I thought at first this mismatch could be attributed to her size, but I later wondered if her relational response to her external environment was more indicative of a history of childhood sexual abuse (Eberhard-Kauchele, 2007) and a learned inability to protect herself. It was as if she was saying through her body, 'I lay myself open, I am not allowed to protect myself, this is what I deserve.'

The group sessions were conducted in the clinic gym – a traditionally 'masculine', linear space, with gym equipment such as benches, weights and medicine balls stacked against the walls, and painted lines on the floor delineating courts for basketball and netball. What resonances and associations might this space have evoked for the group members, with its distinctive, school-education ambience? Did it conjure up fun, success, achievement, a welcome break from sitting at desks and learning, freedom, excitement, team spirit? Or was it the site of humiliation, frustration, boredom, failure, pain and isolation? Each participant's experience would be flavoured by this particular environment.

Our attention to the environment as therapists was first physical, in setting up a space with clear boundaries: chairs placed in a circle, so all participants were able to see each other and both therapists at all times; coloured paper on the door apertures and windows for privacy, and a 'time-out' area just outside the chair circle, furnished with soft blankets. All this helped to 'feminise' the space and, we hoped, enable the women to experience the environment as somewhere they could belong. But my co-lead and I also created this containment psychologically, through our holding presence, emotional availability and consistent attention to time and space boundaries. The creation of a carefully contained environment was, we felt, important in enabling the introduction of male presence to the group. However, there was a disappointing lack of response from the men's ward and in the end only one came forward to join the group.

In the first group session, which the male participant declined to attend, Caroline told us that she 'didn't like men' but said she would be 'okay' with them attending the group as my co-lead and I were there to keep her 'safe'. By contrast, Ayesha, who claimed not to be 'bothered' by the presence of men, spent the first 15 minutes of the subsequent session, when the male participant first attended, tightly bound and coiled like a spring – her body silently revealing what she found difficult to put into words. Yet, two weeks later, both Ayesha and Caroline were readily mirroring the movements of the male participant, and he theirs. The women continued to do so, even after he decided to leave the group, indicating that they were able to hold him in mind and even acknowledge his presence and subsequent absence. Whether this was a benign or threatening presence was ambiguous, yet it clearly made an impact.

We had not set out to create a 'women's group', so the difficulty in attracting and maintaining a male presence raised interesting questions for me. The institution itself emphasised the stereotypical binary distinction between male and female, with its distinct separate locations. It did not seem to me the place where gender fluidity was encouraged or acceptable, and I imagined that masculine stereotypes were powerfully present. The need to demonstrate independence, a reluctance to seek help, and fear of emotional expression and intimacy would all impact negatively on our attempts to recruit men to the group. The medicated numbness that was apparent to me on the men's ward certainly suggested that emotions were better suppressed than expressed, which was in direct opposition to our therapeutic aims in the group.

Using dance movement in a group gives the therapist an opportunity to attune physically with the clients, providing them with a reparative experience of holding at a pre-verbal developmental stage. I wondered if this type of intimate relationship in itself could be a threat to the maintenance of a stereotypical heterosexual masculine image? In addition, our group was dominated both in numbers and authority by women; did this create a potentially threatening or unwelcoming environment for the 'other'? Our attempts to feminise the location might also have proved uncomfortable for men. Containment and constraint are closely aligned, and what is safe for one person may be imprisoning or dangerous for another.

***

Fast forward three years. Today I am taking a very different route to work and have swapped the leafy streets of south London and the Victorian hospital for inner-city north London and a community mental health centre, where I run a weekly movement therapy group for women. My walk from the station feels like a battle. These streets are narrow, crowded and noisy, and are lined with myriad retail outlets, takeaway food shops and cafés, markets and clothing stores. Everywhere there is colour, light, sound and smell – an assault on the senses. There is a high degree of homelessness in the area, and a great deal of poverty. Paradoxically, the area also attracts a huge number of tourists, and hordes of people spill out onto the street at each bus stop. Young and old, rich and poor, people of all cultures and ethnicities gather here. Some are visitors, passing through for an afternoon; for others, the street is literally their home. The route I take requires much twisting and turning of my body, a great deal of muscular effort, and a sophisticated level of awareness to make my way swiftly and safely through this melange.

I arrive at the centre, where they are just finishing up from lunch. The afternoon schedule is a women-only space, so the male service users are preparing to leave. The transition is noisy and chaotic. Unlike the strict protocol and routine of the forensic clinic, here there are no keys, no alarms, no locked doors or 'no-go' areas for service users. Once I enter the community centre, I immediately become part of the dance – staff and service users alike navigating their way through the space.

I head towards the office to collect my bag of props and my CD player, greeting various service users as I do so. I move to greet the shift manager and make her aware of my arrival, but we are interrupted by a service user who needs to speak to her before he leaves. I turn back towards the basement room where I run my weekly group – the room that is mine for the afternoon, the room where I carve out space amid the noise and chaos. There is currently building work taking place outside and I can hear the occasional gruff shouts of construction workers over the bang and clatter of heavy shoes vibrating on the scaffolding platforms.

Inside the room, someone has left a bin liner filled with rubbish and a pile of newspapers, which I remove before covering the windows with coloured paper and placing a sign outside the door stating: 'Session in Progress – Please Do Not Disturb.' Despite this, other service users have from time to time wandered into the room in the middle of a session, looking for a group or a member of staff. I set out four chairs in a circle, and lay out my props – my audio CDs, my swathes of coloured fabric, my colouring pens and paper – switch on the floor lamps and put a box of tissues on a side table. As it is in the basement, the light is dim and the room is cool – a blessing in the blistering heat of summer.

Once the room is ready, I stand in the centre – and breathe. I carry out an internal 'body scan', bringing to awareness and addressing any tension, tightness or muscular holding in my own body. Breathing allows the energy to flow through me once again, as I open myself to feeling after the effortful journey I have taken to reach this space, this place. As I connect with my body, my breath and the ground beneath me, I allow the sounds of the construction work outside the building and the noise of service users inside to slowly recede. This regular routine is my attempt to carve out an internal space of relaxed readiness, awareness and availability to my clients – a place of safety for the women in the group – and to make the internal external. As the custodian of this space for the next 90 minutes, I am aware of the constant dance between internal and external; that my own internal landscape expressed through my own body has the potential to impact the external – and vice versa (Orbach, 2004).

When we began working together, there was some understandable resistance and hesitancy on the part of the women to commit to and invest in the group. This manifested in typical acting-out behaviour, such as arriving late and missing sessions, but was also visible through their movement and use of space in relation to the group. One participant, Suki, spent most of the creative movement process with her eyes closed, seemingly unable to bear being witnessed in her process or to allow herself to be influenced by others. Her movements were small, tight and repetitive and followed a 'sucking' rhythm, akin to the changes in muscular tension of a suckling infant (Kestenberg et al, 1999). Another participant, Beverley, would engage obediently in a basic mirroring exercise in which members take turns in leading and following the other participants, but would then sit apart, just outside the circle, in the closing reflective discussion. Though appearing to be engaged, her body position in relation to the others marked her as an 'outsider'.

Over time, however, as the group members became more comfortable with each other, I began to notice subtle shifts in their overall movement patterns – from small, contained and boundaried to large, expansive and free. Most significantly, their use of the floor increased dramatically over this period. In one particular session, I noticed all three women lying on their backs, legs splayed, knees pointing upwards, and was struck by the strong 'birthing' image that came to mind – an image that was almost sexual in its willing surrender to gravity and to the moment. When I shared this observation and its striking impact in our reflective discussion, Beverley responded: 'You know, it's funny you should say that, because at the time when I was lying on the floor, moving my hips, I remember thinking, "I'm so glad this is a women-only group".' When encouraged to expand on this, she added that there were things she felt 'safe enough' to do and talk about in the group that she would not even contemplate in a mixed group.

To me, the women's increased use of the floor and their relationship to it – crawling, lying, rolling and rocking – indicated a regression to an infantile stage of development, and caused me to reflect on their growing idealisation of the group as a 'safe space', placing me firmly in the role of 'caring mother'. Reflecting further on this in supervision, I realised that this was a necessary stage to work through but that now it was time for the group members to take back responsibility. I needed to support the group members in co-creating firm boundaries in order to provide a robust container for meaningful work, rather than allowing them to continue to project the responsibility onto me. In doing so, I had to be prepared to risk incurring anger, envy and disappointment by refusing to identify with and take on the role of idealised 'mother' (McWilliams & Stein, 1987).

I was also aware of my own responsibility in co-creating the idealised 'safe space', and perhaps my own over-zealousness in attempting to carve this in a decidedly 'female-unfriendly' environment. Perhaps my well-meaning desire to create a 'safe space' for my clients had led me to unwittingly collude with their defences; by focusing intently on security, had I underplayed the importance of challenge and growth? I also wondered how much of my own embodied response to the external environment was being picked up in the transference, leading the women to project an image of the idealised mother who could and would 'protect' them at all costs.

By looking to me to protect them from the outside world and from perceived boundary violations such as interruptions and noise, the women willingly handed over their power to me as custodian of the 'safe space'. While this was expressed verbally in their voiced desire for a 'safe, respectful' space, their bodies told a different story, hinting at unexpressed anger and resentment – in Suki's closed eyes and in Beverley's position outside the circle. 'Negative' emotions were masked by a veil of politeness and obedience. However, this dynamic shifted when one of the women arrived late to a group session. I encouraged the women to express their feelings about the lateness and to reach an agreement as a collective about an acceptable time frame in which to arrive in future. Over the next few weeks, the women gradually expressed their anger, resentment and disappointment – including their anger at me for not holding the boundaries of the group and failing to 'punish' the group member for her poor timekeeping. Through healthy expression of their feelings in response to the lateness and a facilitated discussion around time and space boundaries, the women in the group were able to experience themselves and acknowledge their own role as co-creators of a safe space, and take some of their power back.

The women continued to use the floor in their creative movement process but, over time, they became more actively engaged with each other as a group, rather than individuals, each in their own, meditative bubble. Now, rather than a regression to an infantile state, their use of the floor had a primitive, tribal quality. Rather than lying on their backs with their eyes closed in a state of passive surrender, their bodies were active and vitalised. Their use of vocalisation and body percussion increased; their movements became interspersed with cries, shouts, stamping and clapping. There was also a greater sense of group cohesion, manifested through shared rhythms, movement synchrony and voice.

Psychologist and mythologist Sharon Blackie describes women's search for home within our environment and the power of connecting to the ground in an embodied way:

> Unable to belong to any particular place, we so often find ourselves unable to belong to the world, from which as a consequence we hold ourselves separate... We spend our lives searching for meaning in ourselves, engaged in deep conversations with our 'inner child'... when so much of the meaning we need is beneath our feet... We badly need grounding: we need to find our anchor in place, wherever it is that we live. (Blackie, 2016: 283)

In finding their anchor and their ground, the women were beginning to find their power, and their voices as a consequence, and to co-create their own safe space by establishing a sense of *belonging* within the group and the therapy space and the wider environment. They were beginning to experience the group as a home for their pain, their sadness, their fear and their fury as well as their joy, their love, their femininity and their vulnerability.

They were able to shift from identifying expressions of anger as masculine and aggressive – and therefore dangerous and 'unsafe' and to be repressed and denied – to finding healthy forms of expression through movement, voice and creative symbolism. More importantly, they were increasingly able to recognise the role that they each played in creating and holding a safe space together, one that enabled exploration, play, creativity and freedom.

The notion of a 'safe space' is centrally important in psychotherapy; it is seen as the necessary condition to enable a client to move beyond their characteristic defences and grasp the possibility of change. This is a space that we recognise can be created, or co-created, through the quality of relating, in the context of certain physical environments. It would be hard, for example, to create a safe and containing space on a motorway verge. Having said that, there are certain moments in time – when the motorway is closed, perhaps – when it might be possible to create this space, sitting quietly in a circle with no interruptions, on a bright clear day with the sun shining and the birds singing. The point is that space and time cannot be parted – a fact that is well established in physics, but often overlooked in favour of yet another binary construction. Space is often perceived as empty, passive (female), whereas (masculine) time is moving, energetic and dynamic (Massey, 2013).

Shortly before I launched my group, a brief psycho-educational programme for women survivors of abuse had been hastily relocated from the community centre, as the ongoing construction work outside the building, carried out by men, had led the organisers to deem it an 'inappropriate environment' for such a client group. The 'passive' space had been intruded upon, at particular times of day, by 'energetic' male power. My attempts to protect the dance movement group and draw a safe boundary around them were a way of resisting this male dominance; only over time did it become possible to allow and express 'masculine' characteristics within the group.

My challenge as a female dance therapist working with women is to create a 'safe-enough' space that enables exploration and expression of vulnerability while also managing the projection of idealised mother and providing a level of rigour required for meaningful and sustainable change. The recognition in the group that space could be co-created, that stereotypical gendered boundaries could be transgressed, was a therapeutic movement from old attitudes and behaviours to new possibilities.

On reflection, the construction site next door was a powerful element in the group experience. It is a common, clichéd occurrence for a woman to walk past a building site and be whistled or shouted at by men. Women are sexually appraised and commented on by heterosexual men in many situations, but the building site scenario is one of the most ubiquitous. Women often remark on their sense of invisibility as they age – a recognition of the pervasive sense of scrutiny experienced when they were a younger, overtly sexual person.

This heterosexual masculine gaze impacts on the bodily awareness of those women being looked at and has physical consequences – we draw in our stomach, toss our head, thrust forward our chest, or put our head down and walk more quickly, hunching the shoulders, for example. The gaze is an expression of social power, the entitlement to judge and comment. It affects self-confidence and self-identity.

Of course, the one looking is not always a heterosexual male. A culture that objectifies and sexualises the other is inevitably internalised; women look at women, men look at men and, relatively recently, women openly appraise and comment on men's bodies. This could be seen as a sign of growing gender equality. However, it is questionable whether women looking at men's bodies produces the same effects as vice versa. Do men feel abashed, cover up, walk away quickly? Or is the gaze perceived as flattering and flirtatious, where the power relations remain the same rather than become inverted?

We learn to handle our bodies though complex internalised perceptions of what others see when they look at us. It seems to me that, stereotypically, women expect to be the 'object' and heterosexual males the subject, the ones who can look and appraise. The presence of the onlookers from the construction site, whether real or imagined, played an important part in the life of the group, although we were not conscious of this dynamic at the time. As Beverley explored her feelings of 'safety' in the women-only group, she spoke of her self-consciousness about her body, her large breasts and her rounded belly, and explained that, in a mixed group, she would feel inhibited in her movements: 'I'd be worried they [the men] would be looking at me and judging me.' Though her words contained the implicit assumption that the women in the group would not be looking at and judging her body, they also hint at the power dynamic at play in men looking at female bodies and who has ownership of the 'voyeuristic' gaze.

In exploring the social construction of space and gender, Martina Löw (2006: 127) notes that 'the constraining, almost compulsive gaze men cast at female bodies is always bound up in a complex of power and knowledge'. She cites Kaufman (1996), who uses the public beach as a pertinent example of this power dynamic at play. He discusses the intuitive behaviour of female topless sunbathers, and how, through a series of careful, often unconscious rituals, women on the beach create a 'safe-enough' space to minimise the boundary-violating impact of the male gaze. One of these, it is noted, is to lie flat and remain immobile while topless. Though breast-baring is an 'act of emancipation', the price to be paid for this so-called liberation, it seems, is the body's immobility:

> It is precisely this exposure of their bodies that now drives women into passivity... The body becomes what space no longer wishes to be: rigid and immobile. (Löw, 2006: 130)

The shift that the women in the group made from lying flat on their backs, in a state of passive surrender in their own private meditative spaces, to a more active, vitalised, cohesive and expansive form indicated to me, more than anything, their intention to transgressively 'genderise' the space through their body movements and claim it as their own. Their use of the body (including the collective 'group body') as an active agent in the space also served to challenge the traditional notion of the feminine as empty and passive, of women as 'objects' in space and passive recipients of the dominant male gaze rather than active co-creators and producers of that space.

***

The use of body movement and dance as a form of creative expression and communication in groups offers a deeper layer of understanding of the unconscious processes taking place at both individual and group level, in relationship with others. The moving, dancing body, given the freedom to express itself fully, offers opportunity to access thoughts, feelings and memories for which words cannot easily be found, to dive deep beneath the surface and to make the unconscious conscious (Taylor, 2007).

Creative body movement provides a direct pathway into the internal landscape. However, we are who we are in the context of others, and we are continually shaped by our external environments (Rose, 2016). Rather than the dance enabling us simply to dive deep and excavate unconscious material, bringing it to the surface of consciousness, this dance was a fluid one between the internal and the external. My experience of being with and moving alongside the women in both groups as they traversed their own pathways and routes via their dancing bodies, also gave me a direct experience of the environments they inhabited and navigated. My own countertransference, experienced somatically, to the places and spaces in which the work took place, was and continues to be a powerful indicator of this dance between the internal and external landscape. What happens 'in here' reflects what happens 'out there' – in relationships, in the family, in organisations, in communities and in society. Our dance together offers a bridge between two worlds, as we continue to bring the outside in and the inside out.

## References

Blackie S (2016). *If Women Rose Rooted: the journey to authenticity and belonging.* London: September Publishing.

Eberhard-Kaechele M (2007). The regulation of interpersonal relationships by means of shape flow: a psychoeducational intervention for traumatised individuals. In: Koch S, Bender S (eds). *Movement Analysis: the legacy of Laban, Bartenieff, Lamb and Kestenberg.* Berlin: Logos Verlag (pp203–211).

Kaufmann J-C (1996). *Frauenkörper–Männerblicke*. Konstanz: UVK. Cited in: Löw M (2006). The social construction of space and gender. *European Journal of Women's Studies 13*(2): 119–133.

Kestenberg J, Loman S, Lewis P, Sossin M (1999). *The Meaning of Movement: developmental and clinical perspectives of the Kestenberg Movement Profile*. New York, NY: Brunner-Routledge.

Koch S, Bender S (eds) (2007). *Movement Analysis: the legacy of Laban, Bartenieff, Lamb and Kestenberg*. Berlin: Logos Verlag.

Laban R (1966). Choreutics (L Ullman, ed). London: MacDonald and Evans.

Löw M (2006). The social construction of space and gender. *European Journal of Women's Studies 13*(2): 119–133.

Massey D (2013). *Space, Place and Gender*. Chichester: Wiley & Sons.

McWilliams N, Stein J (1987). Women's groups led by women: the management of devaluing transferences. *International Journal of Group Psychotherapy 37*(2): 139–153.

Orbach S (2004). What can we learn from the therapist's body? *Attachment and Human Development 6*(2): 141–500.

Rose C (2017). *Where we come from: place and colour*. [Blog.] Chris Rose. https://chrisrose.me/2017/03/ (accessed 9 April 2019).

Rose C (2016). Walking together. *Therapy Today 27*(10): 22–25.

Stern DN (1985). The sense of a subjective self II: affect attunement. In: Stern DN. *The Interpersonal World of the Infant: a view from psychoanalysis and developmental psychology*. New York, NY: Basic Books (pp138–161).

Taylor J (2007). Authentic movement: the body's path to consciousness. *Body, Movement and Dance in Psychotherapy 2*(1): 47–56.

# 2 | Taking space
## Jane Samuels

The city is a complex space: a living, layered confluence of history, present and future. It is at once personal and social. Its inhabitants live out their intimate narratives, which build into the stories of streets, neighbourhoods and boroughs. This is the scaffolding with which a city's history, attitude and spirit is constructed. We learn that these narrow, terraced streets housed our grandparents and their grandparents. We see the smooth curve of worn stones and we can clearly hear their footsteps crossing the threshold. We hear the stories about their communities and we feel them all: leaning against back-yard walls, jostling noisily through football crowds, propping up bars in pubs that have long been empty plots, each one of them a cell in our communal bloodstream.

I'm gulping black coffee from my 'Salford' mug. It's cheaply produced, not worth the six pounds it cost me. Printed on its white surface is a list of black, capitalised words: 'SALFORD. CROSS LANE. CRESCENT. REGENT ROAD. HANKINSON STREET. WHIT LANE. ELLOR STREET.' I only know where four of these streets are, but Salford is where I'm from, and these words on a cheap mug are far more than a list of place names. I was born in Hope Hospital (STOTT LANE) and my grandparents grew tomatoes and made paper bird cages with me in Salford's red brick terraces, where my Mum grew up, shy and lovely (LANGWORTHY ROAD). I learned to ride a bicycle in Buile Hill Park (ECCLES OLD ROAD), and when my parents moved us away from Salford and from Manchester, I took those names with me, printed through the marrow of my bones as though through a stick of rock. My mother and her mother came from a family of storytellers. The tales of family they passed on were really tales of the city. Details change, but the spirit remains. In this way, the city was given to me: a gift from birth of redbrick and swagger, my head and heart filled with its ghosts until I could feel the cool shadow of the Langworthy pub fall across the pavement long after its last brick was gone.

My dad was the son of Jewish immigrants. He was born in Manchester, but his roots in the city were shallower than mine. His grandparents spoke only Yiddish, and at school and on the streets, in his yarmulke, he was forced to fight for his right to a place in the city. Where my mother gave me Salford, he gave me Manchester, Prestwich and potato kugel – not just a food, but a glimpse of my heritage, each mouthful a common experience with grandparents I never met and a direct link to the streets they walked (CHEETHAM HILL). In Blackley, I lived five minutes away from my grandmother's grave in the Jewish cemetery (ROCHDALE ROAD), and I have never once visited it. Every few years, local Nazis scrawl the graves with swastikas and smash the stones, and every time I resolve to go but do not. They remind me that, to some, this city still isn't mine; that even for those dug into the earth, among the foundations of its earliest settlements, there is still a battle raging to belong.

From the newcomers who have to make their own stories and build their own mental maps to those carrying histories of their ancestors through a constantly modernising city, we all are jostling for place. The very nature of the city is to push back: to isolate, confuse and disorientate. Urban space can be hard edged and violent, and there are times in which it becomes necessary for each of us to take the city by storm. This chapter deals with that battle for belonging and the search for an urban existence that is authentic. Using the English city of Manchester as a basis, it explores the ways in which walking through the city may help us build and reassert deep connections with urban space and with the people we share it with. This in turn can develop our emotional landscapes, deepen our roots and create places that can emotionally nourish and 'hold' us. The chapter will use these terms, 'taking space' and 'holding space', to represent this cyclical relationship in which the individual 'takes space' to create a city of their own, and in turn the now personalised city 'holds that space' to become a place of growth, thought and examination. It explores how women in particular may freely move through the hostile city and learn to take the space.

## Taking space: the power of walking

In counselling, training, conflict resolution and wider mental health fields, practitioners are likely to be familiar with Carl Rogers and his work on active listening (Rogers & Farson, 1957). Rogers, regarded as the father of person-centred counselling, explains that, if we suspend our own beliefs and needs, we are able to let others openly express theirs. He suggests that judgement (whether critical or favourable) can make free expression difficult. He asks that in active listening the listener looks for, and responds to, the total meaning: both the content of the message and the feelings that go with it. He reminds the listener to note the smallest of cues: the facial expression that suggests further meaning or the tone of voice that indicates emotion or urgency. This process creates a space in which another feels safe to express themselves freely and fully. It allows individuals to self-actualise and aids groups to improve their cohesion and understanding. It is a way, as Rogers rather beautifully puts it, of 'demonstrat[ing] a spirit which genuinely respects the potential worth of the individual, which considers his sights and trusts his capacity for self-direction…' (Rogers & Farson, 1957: 25).

In psychogeography, this quest for self-actualisation is woven into urban walking practice. These ideas extend beyond purely human interactions and into the fabric of our cities. The Situationist International describes this process as:

> ... the study of the precise laws and the specific effects of the geographical environment, consciously organised or not, on the emotions and behaviour of individuals. (Debord, 1955)

Psychogeography asks where the human mind and body sit in urban spaces and what freedoms these spaces provide to self-actualise. It asks how we can measure individual worth against a commercial idealisation of progress, what structures – both social and geographical – may bind us, and how we can make ourselves free. Psychogeographers ask who holds the power in private and public spaces, and how (and if) that power can be equalised. They ask to what extent are we allowed our most basic biological needs: how easy is it, for example, to sit, to urinate, to ask for and receive help, to move freely and to be unafraid to create our narratives and build our communities? It is the cyclical exploration of urban cause and human effect.

The city is not a safe space and does not give room gladly. There is no active listening to be found from stone and steel and, often, very little offered by the councils and corporations that construct the streets and squares. The urban environment can be isolating, anonymous and lonely. It can be aggressive and hostile. A walker may perceive judgement in the gaze of a passer-by, a bored security guard, an assistant in an expensive shop. Blinking, revolving billboards flash blinding smiles and ask: are you sure you're quite good enough? Thin enough? Is that old watch on your wrist expensive enough? It's easy to become faceless in the crowds and dwarfed by the stone.

Psychogeography suggests that the act of walking, of movement, through the city offers a means for reconnection. Day-to-day walking in the city is often purposeful, with a destination in mind: people in the city rush from A to B and seldom stop to consider the streets they walk. The Situationists contended that an aimless walk, without route or destination, could open up the wonders of the city and make the walker take notice, get a little lost, marvel a little. The '*dérive*' or 'drift' they described bimbles and wanders; it takes notice of detail and it observes the rhythm of the city and the walker's place within it (Debord, 1956).

In his 1967 publication *The Society of the Spectacle*, Debord uses a Marxist grounding to explore the ways in which capitalist players employ spectacle as a form of social control. The spectacle commodifies and so neutralises radical thought and sets a social agenda defined by Baudrillard's hyper-reality: a constant bombardment of signs and symbols that are not 'real' life but more glamorous, more enticing (Baudrillard, 1998). It is a process of entrancement and seduction: we are pulled this way and that, like kittens chasing tinsel.

We are bombarded by moving billboards, interactive adverts and screens ever-present in our hands offering algorithmic adverts, tailor-made political discourse, carefully packaged soundbites, constant distraction and increasing insularisation. We are sold hyper-real versions of ourselves and each other: carefully packaged and presented materials from which to construct our self-image. Advertisers have even repackaged our demonstrations against inequality, commodified the imagery of protest and used it to sell us their products. We have become busier, more anxious, more numerous and more distracted now than Debord could ever have imagined.

Debord considered the spectre of terrorism, too, to be a tool of the spectacle, whereby mass media coverage and the fear that comes from daily pleas for vigilance becomes a method of control. In a post-9/11 world, it is possible to understand that there is a true and increased need for vigilance. Kosovic (2011) contends that the new global terror threat outgrows Debord's position, offering very real threat and creating an urban spectacle of its own. We are newly, globally torn between the spectacle of terror itself and the media portrayal that rewards global terrorism with its attention. In Manchester, we have too much experience of this on which to draw, and this chapter will revisit the spectacle of terror and the ways in which walking and being in the city has been used to diminish it.

Today, in our cities full of disconnect and fear, the need for grounding is more necessary than ever, and I consider 'active walking' an accessible term for the 'drift'. Borrowing from Rogers, 'active walking' describes a process of moving through the city that takes notice. The walker is forced to make new decisions, think about actions and movement and become aware of affect and effect. In Joyce's *Ulysses*, Stephen Dedalus says metaphorically of Ulysses' epic journey: 'We walk through ourselves... meeting robbers, ghosts, giants, old men, young men, wives, widows, brothers-in-love. But always meeting ourselves' (Joyce, 1922/2000: 273). In active walking, it is possible to make epic journeys in the most familiar places and, in so doing, cut through the spectacle to find something authentic. In the memory-enhancing technique the 'method of loci', imagined movement through place triggers a string of pre-planted memories (Foer, 2011). So too, physical movement through place uncovers new thoughts, feelings and ways of being. In forging deep relationships with place that foster a sense of knowing and belonging, place itself may support our self-actualisation: our creativity, curiosity, understanding of self and our position in place and time. It might be possible, as we set out into the city, for the city to hold the space.

## Taking space: finding authenticity in the spectacle

On 22 May 2017, at 10.31pm, Salaman Abedi walked into the foyer at The Manchester Arena. It is a transitory place, full of doors to other places. People use it to wait, grab limp fast food, travel through between concerts and trains. Abedi used it to detonate a suicide bomb that would propel metal into human bodies, mostly those of young women, killing 22. The city filled with ambulances, rumour and fear. We checked on each other across our networks: a map of our people and their likely proximity to the bomb flashing through our heads. Message after message spread out across the phone networks and internet, passing news, asking questions and searching already for our loved ones – the beginnings of something terrible that we did not yet understand.

Ariana Grande is a singer known for her feminist message who supports the free expression of female sexuality. She brought her 'Dangerous Woman' tour to Manchester: a message of empowerment to her predominantly female teen fan base. It is impossible to know Abedi's thinking behind his choice of target, but as images of the dead were released to the media – smiling, shining girls with braces, glasses, Snapchat filter flowers around their heads – it was difficult to forget how unsafe it can be to be a Dangerous Woman in public space. When women are seen to reject traditional patriarchal norms, they make themselves visible to those who uphold those beliefs. This was Kosovic's spectacle of terrorism: the shock reminder that, where there is perceived dissent to an oppressive doctrine, violence, chaos and fear may follow.

The week following the attack was full of false alarms and chaos. The police raided houses and flats all over the city, blowing off the doors as they went. The city felt alien and disturbing. I worked at the university while helicopters thrummed overhead; I drank coffee to the sound of explosions and bought my groceries in the presence of militaristic police brandishing giant automatic guns. There was an acute awareness of where our bodies were in the city in relation to the scene of the violence and, as the city's hurrying pedestrians neared the stadium, they grew quieter and slower until, in the streets around the Corn Exchange and the Arndale through to St Ann's Square, there was silence. The city chatter was gone, replaced with starling song and distant traffic noise. Walkers reflected the geography of this cyclical spectacle of violence and response, and so doing, we became a part of it.

Global news corporations descended on the city and amplified the fear and chaos, repackaging it into soundbites and iconic images. It fetishised our unity and strength and it stretched out its hand to feed the next terrorist: *Look what you could do. We'll make you famous.*

The day after the attack was a Tuesday. Victoria Station and some roads were closed; the city became an island of silent commuters. Buying newspapers, ordering coffee, people openly cried. Still they walked, worked and ate, hugged and talked to strangers in the queue. I walked through the streets and caught the eyes of passers-by: we nodded, said hello, where usually we would rush past, mutually unheeded. We were finding a real and raw connection that broke through the spectacle and remains the thing most of us remember best about the spirit of those few days. The terror spectacle had been so great, it was forcing us blinkingly out into the streets and towards one another: a raw response, unmitigated yet by mass media.

By five o'clock, there were processions forming, moving together from every part of the city: post-work and mid-shift and homeless folk. Tributaries joined the streams until they were five deep, silent and moving together from every part of the city.

There was no sway, no Manchester swagger: just the sound of footfall, the gentle rustle of moving bodies. This moment, this walking together on our streets under the gaze of no one but each other, was a key moment in the reclamation of the city. It was a pilgrimage back to ourselves.

Albert Square is dotted with statues: James Fraser, a bishop and vocal anti-Darwin exponent; John Bright, a radical Quaker and Liberal who fought hard against the Corn Laws; Oliver Haywood, a banker and philanthropist. As the stream of Mancunian life entered the square, these varied and various Manchester men (women are scarce among Manchester's totems) became part of the crowd, their eyes fixed like our own. Concurrent histories met together in a single shared moment of silent witnessing. *We are here.* Faces marked with tears: the city is its people. We held the space. We took the city back from the terrorists and the armed police. Local poet Tony Walsh's reading of 'This is the place' held its resonance long after the speeches in the square. Powerfully rooted in place, it linked us beautifully to our accents and our folk, our shared experiences that shape identity and reinforce belonging. When the speeches were done, a spontaneous football-terrace chant broke out: 'Man-Chest-er! Man-Chest-er! Man-Chest-er!' The city is a living confluence of stone, steel, glass and flesh: people are the city, and in this act, the city held the space. People found their friends in the crowd and went to the pubs: the places Mancunians have gathered to talk, laugh and cry together for hundreds of years. We went to drink in those tiled rooms to welcome ghosts, remember roots and reaffirm our belonging.

Then the media spectacle swung into full action. In St Ann's Square, where people had begun spontaneously laying tributes, an impenetrable ring of global press sprung up like some great, sucking insect: bristling furry booms and spikey rigs. As people gathered to lay flowers and balloons, they were forced to form a queue, each stepping through a small gap in the wall of press, one by one, a hundred cameras tracking every move. Already, on some level, under the gaze of the world, these small acts of personal and community tribute were transformed into a performative act; people were forced to self-consciously perform for the spectacle, and so became it. The mourning process on the streets was repackaged and beamed to the world.

I visited the tributes after the press were finally gone, and before the city workers began to so carefully clear them away. Much is written about public displays of community mourning, and sometimes rather sniffily questions its purpose and authenticity. After a week, the tributes filled St Ann's Square in its entirety. It was breathtakingly huge and silent, and instantly clear that this was the physical representation of a community's heartbreak. Closer, individual thoughts and feelings became visible. People wrote their pain with the flowers and offered them to the streets. I became aware of two women to the left of me. They walked on crutches, their limbs bandaged. Their visible skin was marked with still-healing wounds made by flying shrapnel, and they were quietly sobbing. As we around them silently realised the weight of that moment, each of us found ourselves crying freely with them. People reached out their hands to strangers and held them. It was a moment of deep community, mutual support and connection to each other, and to our city. We held the space.

## Taking space in hostile cultures

It is possible to see, then, that the city can be both disorientating, alienating and sometimes frightening, and it can offer people new depths of connection, both to place and to people. After the Manchester Arena bomb, it was people's connection to the city's bricks and mortar and to the shared experiences in the shadow of those stones that helped us process the aftermath, just as other human actors (in this case, the spectacle of media) acted to alienate people from their own mourning process. There are other barriers to connection and self-actualisation in the city, more mundane than acts of terror but daily and pernicious.

In 1950, 79% of the UK's population was living in cities. That figure is expected to rise to 92.2% by 2030. In Manchester, the 2001 census recorded 11,689 inhabitants in the 'Central' Manchester area, and still more shuttle to and from satellite towns in the commuter belt (Champion, 2014). Add the steadily growing 115 million visitors a year to the city centre, and then consider this: Manchester city centre currently has just one public toilet. The implications of this are immediately clear: people must pay coffee shops and bars for the right to their most basic biological functions or enter privately owned shopping centres or the few remaining security-protected libraries in order to relieve themselves. If a person can wait long enough and travel far enough to find a free and accessible toilet, they may still find that barriers are in place. Those judged to be 'inappropriate', perhaps because they are trans, disabled, struggling with mental health or homelessness, may not carry sufficient social currency to be allowed simply to pee in privacy. It is difficult to imagine a more basic form of biological self-expression, or a more easily understood need, that is so controlled in the city by commerce, infrastructure and power. Homeless people all over the city navigate areas of safety and danger. City leaders install spikes to dig into bodies that need to sleep. They remove benches where the old and tired need rest. It is the hard edge of stone against flesh, and this powerplay affects us at fundamental biological, psychological and behavioural levels. In the built environment then, it becomes necessary to occupy space not easily won, and who you are and what you need will dictate how difficult that might be.

Manchester's Loiterers Resistance Movement (LRM) has been playing in the city for over a decade (see Chapter 6). They enjoy a monthly drift through the city that embraces creativity and exploration. Walkers may follow directions suggested by a wind-blown paper, conduct a treasure hunt for urban signs and symbols, or go in search of hidden rivers. It is about noticing and cherishing the small details of the city, learning old stories, weaving new ones and, in so doing, creating personal and shared cities that belong to us, *and in which we belong*. Adults mostly, who remember that there is great worth in play, they have made and eaten cake maps of their favourite buildings and played games of urban tag. Morag Rose, founder of the LRM, places at its heart a profound love of the city and its people, a genuine concern for equity and a healthy wariness of gentrification. In her fight against corporate drabness and in defence of magic and play, Rose embodies a great deal of the psychogeographical ideal, and yet, as a woman in the field, she faces a particular problem.

In practice and literature, psychogeography has been overwhelmingly white and male. As its ideas have regained popularity during the past decade, it is the voices of white, able-bodied men that appear in newspaper columns and radio commentaries. Morag Rose (2017) sets Baudelaire's *flâneur* – the white, male 'saunterer' who wanders the streets, freely observing – against the female experience of being looked at and appraised by heterosexual men in the street. This 'male gaze' judges and objectifies women. Street harassment, sexual assault and the rape of women in the city means that women are unable to walk streets unhindered or unseen and must make decisions about where they are and are not safe. Rose asks if it is possible for the carefree female wanderer, the *flâneuse*, to really exist when their experience is often so different to that of their male counterpart. Rose conducted a series of walking interviews in Manchester to gather accounts of women's urban experiences. During her research, men regularly interrupted her interviews. These interruptions ranged from offering unsolicited advice to yelling sexual abuse, the most sexually overt of which was 'Fuck her in the pussy!', yelled into her microphone, before the man ran off down the street. Only one woman interrupted her during the course of the research; she wanted to apologise in case she had been talking too loudly as they recorded. Women can find it difficult to take the space.

Women's urban experience in the city is influenced by the architecture; the towering glass and dirtied stone create quiet back streets, places where a woman can be followed and grabbed. Our experience is affected by the planting in park spaces that allows for hidden spots, and the darkness of broken lamp posts between pools of light. Women's social lives are shaped by the need to travel home alone at 3am, to the heart of a housing estate, and having to decide between a quick-paced walk along sleeping streets or a single, taxi-driving stranger. On busy daytime streets and crowded public transport, women experience harassment, sexual innuendo and assault. A woman on her own might find herself splitting the city into spaces that are safe and those that are hostile, restricting herself to walking down the main streets and missing the wonderful intrigue of alleyways. Simple acts such as choosing where and what to drink in the city are affected by women's perception and experience of the physicality, geography, culture and accessibility of urban space. A woman might choose to enter cafés on her own but perhaps not bars, because the unspoken rules of each are widely different and subtly gendered. The threat of street harassment, violence or rape can shape the movements of women and their freedom to move, dress, travel in and engage with the urban setting through decisions that are made and normalised as a part of everyday life. The spectacle feeds this perception: hyper-real billboard bodies are perfect, desirable and endlessly available on the streets.

Where governments, corporations or oppressive ideologies exert too much control, there is often a counter reaction to claim back the space. Globally, people are using protest and play in order to assert their right to place. In the UK, protesters have responded to anti-homeless spikes by covering them with cushions and blankets, offering a softer place to rest. This simple, gentle action has resulted in spikes removed by councils and businesses in Manchester and other cities. Disabled activists have taken to the streets to demand better access to public transport and urban infrastructure. Women too, have long used urban spaces, first to

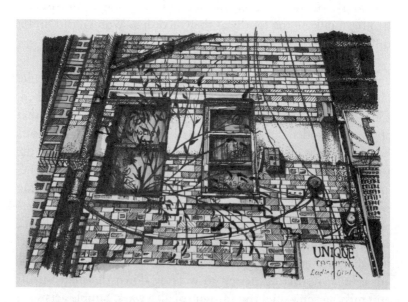

protest their lack of rights, and later, as those rights became law, to demand equal treatment. In the late 19th century, the suffragettes used street protest to call for women in Britain to have the right to vote. They used a range of sometimes violent actions, in which the taking up of physical space was a common theme. Marchers placed their bodies in urban spaces, making them hyper-visible, and sometimes, when they shackled themselves to railings, immovable. Their presence cut through the usual business of urban life and forced people to confront and consider their defiance. In so doing, they made their struggle a part of the urban experience and the social consciousness.

These narratives differ in the context of global culture and basic needs. In early 2018, women in Iran risked arrest and assault when they protested laws that compelled them to wear headscarves in public. Images circulated of the women were incredibly powerful: they stood silently in the streets, bare-headed, often alone, on benches, bollards and pedestals, their headscarves tied to sticks held in front of them. These were acts of both frightening vulnerability and incredible strength as they exerted their right to full and free self-expression in urban space, and in so doing silently asserted their political identity and ideological community and began a global conversation.

The act of reclaiming space can be seen in the names of some protest movements: 'Take back the night' is a global movement that sees women marching, attending rallies and vigils at night, asserting their presence in the city after dark and demanding freedom from abuse. The 'slut walks' began in Toronto, Canada, to protest a police officer's suggestion that women should 'avoid dressing like sluts' if they didn't want to be sexually assaulted. As Morag Rose's research so starkly illustrates (many of her participants were professionally dressed for their work in the city), modest dress does not save women from street harassment or assault, and the 'slut walks' serve to remind the city's inhabitants that women should be free of abuse, however they dress.

The LightUp Collective was the 2017 brainchild of Manchester Metropolitan University students Zuzanna Niska and Jess Mallard, in response to regular sexual attacks on the student population.[1] The pair ran workshops and consultations and collaborated with local police and the students union to empower female students to use the city safely and to challenge the male violence they experienced on the streets. They organised night-time events where they filled dark and quiet places in the city with light: strings of bulbs wrapped around handrails and hanging from trees, and invited students into them, to share experiences and thoughts and to enjoy being present in the night-time city in places where they had previously felt fear. Physical theatre group RashDash held a similar event on the night-time streets of Leeds.[2] They performed *The Darkest Corners*, written to highlight violence against women and share stories of resistance, music and a visceral celebration of the city.

It seems unlikely that these fleeting happenings offer any meaningful deterrent to attackers or abusers, but they do provide a space in which women can be supported, openly dialogue and, if only for one evening, freely place their bodies in areas of urban space that they were previously afraid to enter. In each instance of resistance or creative walking in the streets, protest or play, people identify and strengthen their connection to place and their community ties.

## Belonging in the city: personal narratives

Psychogeography is a personal as well as social investigation. My own connection to the city has been one of community, learning, teaching, political protest, conflict, and occasional arrest. We have played and danced here, running through the streets dressed as zombies and foxes, full of political idealism and a deep and abiding love for our people and our places. The streets connect me to my community and history and, as I walk, places unravel their histories as new pages are added. As for so many other women, my experiences are punctuated with street harassment and sexual assaults, and I am forced to consider my movements and amend my maps. I will close this chapter with a personal narrative: a

---

1. LightUp. www.facebook.com/LightUpFallowfield/ (accessed 27 April 2018).
2. RashDash. www.rashdash.co.uk/thedarkestcorners/ (accessed 27 April 2018).

moment of psychogeography in action, when my city held the space.

We received news that my mum had cancer on the same day that I learned the long-expected closure of my workplace was unavoidable: a day of unpleasant confirmations. That same day, walking through Manchester, away from the work announcement and towards my mum's news, I heard a BANG! just behind me, so loud it stopped me dead and spun me around. An unconscious man was lying at my feet, his eyes flickering white. A foot swung and connected hard with the side of his head, already bleeding from a perfectly straight gash that travelled from the top of his forehead to the bridge of his nose. He had been slammed against the metal edge of a hotel sign, one that I knew covered a piece of graffiti that my husband had scrawled there in his less civic-minded but more idealistic days. The graffiti had said 'Unity' and I could still see the bottom of the 'Y' poking below the metal. As the attacker ran, I crouched next to the prone man and placed my hands on each side of the wound to push the edges together. I could see the pink of his skull, briefly, before I pressed down, hard. Unity, indeed.

The man had taken spice: a synthetic cannabinoid that has been sweeping through Manchester's ever-growing homeless population. It can make people aggressive and uninhibited, and he had darted through the city, frightening and threatening, taking his space too, in his way, but taking far too much. He threatened the wrong man. When he came to, he was raving and violent: he poked his fingers at the wound, opening it up and undoing my work. He attacked the ambulance crew that had arrived and ran back towards Canal Street, leaving a blood trail for the police to follow. The paramedic crew and I sat in their ambulance, trying to clean off the worst of the blood. 'Are you alright love? That was a bit of an ordeal.' This was a city I knew: conflict and violence felt a lot like home.

I took the train back to the hills. Seated at the kitchen table, I drew a long breath: one last moment before the world lurched around, and I called Mum. I sat listening as she cried, my stomach filled with gritstone, and an hour later, I was heading back to the city again, needing the streets.

When I need grounding or new understanding, I walk. As I go, the city unfolds whispered doorway conversations, broken windows, 3am slaps across the face. It shows me things I had forgotten. Step after fast step, I think about the man with the gash across his head, making his own stormy progress through the streets. My husband walks beside me, keeping pace, saying nothing. He holds the space.

We reach Ancoats, stepping through beer cans and old papers. Past Shudehill, where ancestors, dead before my birth, sold brushes. I know them as I pass and think about impermanence and the fading marks we make. We march on to the Corn Exchange, once a wonderful pile of ornate tile and wrought iron, now mostly sterile chrome and glass. During my teens, it was filled with ramshackle market stalls of books and velvet dresses. I smell its dust, warm wood and old pages as I go.

Faster, past the broken fountains and up by the fur shops that I have stood outside in protest a hundred times, talking, dancing, fighting. We're flying through the city now, taking long, fast strides, arms slashing razor-arcs in the air. As we go, the city blurs: glass after glass after stone, my reflection repeated and refracted.

We move past the site of Peterloo where, in 1819, protesting Mancunians were massacred by the Yeomanry. Mancunians have always fought, for good or ill. Up, out of the heart of one Manchester and into another: the universities and the place I learned to live by myself. My new, unsupervised life blossomed here, and the city held me. I found my tribe and it held us together, too.

I'm frightened I won't be strong enough to support her. I'm scared of the waiting and the operations, the steady electronic beep. I'm frightened of the blood tests and the murmuring chemo room, where people drink coffee, eat neat NHS cheese sandwiches, read *Chat* and knit babies' hats while quietly and mundanely fighting for their lives.

We walk past the pub where my husband and I met. He walks silently with me now, a lifetime later, a million beers after. A thousand nights of carefree dancing until the morning city found us awake still and walking, a little wilder and a little more knowing. All of that – before this.

In this way, we perform a tightening circle as I speak out my fear, spilling it out into the roads and down the alleys; spitting it behind me on the wet stone and listening for the city's reply. There is a spot on the York-stone slabs that is still stained with blood, only half washed away by a doorman, who has seen it all before. Great splashes of browned blood lead away from it: a line on the life-map of another person's city. At the point where our maps converged in time and place, where I held his head together with my hands, I stop. I see my form reflected in the windows above. I breathe out. This is not OK. There is already an awakening sense that I am changing forever. But... 'OK,' I say. 'I think I'm ready.'

It is clear, then, I hope, that in great and small acts of defiance, creativity, compassion, play and story-building, it is possible for people to mould a city to make it intimately their own. They can use these connections with the streets to be heard, to challenge hostilities, build communities, navigate shared traumas and express themselves more freely in the urban environment. In taking space, forging deep connection with the streets and the people who share them, it is possible to create an environment that supports personal and emotional development and exploration.

Claiming our place in the city is a battle that might be embodied by a challenge or a violent act: a need to escape its hardness with a drug or a kick in the head. It can be as small a gesture as walking an unfamiliar street. It should not be romanticised, because homelessness, disability, sexual violence and deprivation are realities for so many. There is push and pull between belonging and alienation, and sometimes we all take too much and give too little. My city looks similar to yours but belongs to no one else. We build armies out of ghosts and add their numbers to the communities we build. Our cities become personalised maps of past, present and future in which we deeply belong. We take the space.

## References

Baudrillard J (1998). Simulacra and simulations. In: Poster M (ed). *Jean Baudrillard: selected writings*. Stanford, CA: Stanford University Press.

Champion T (2014). *People in Cities: the numbers*. Future of Cities working paper. Foresight Project. London: Government Office for Science.

Debord G (1967/1992). *The Society of the Spectacle* (K Knabb trans). London: Rebel Press.

Debord G (1956). Theory of the dérive (K Knabb, trans). *Les Lèvres Nues 9*: November. www.cddc.vt.edu/sionline/si/theory.html (accessed 25 April 2018).

Debord G (1955). Introduction to a critique of urban geography (K Knabb, trans). *Les Lèvres Nues 6*; September. www.cddc.vt.edu/sionline/presitu/geography.html (accessed 25 April 2018).

Foer J (2011). *Moonwalking with Einstein: the art and science of remembering everything*. New York, NY: Penguin Press.

Joyce J (1922/2000). *Ulysses*. London: Penguin Books.

Kosovic M (2011). Revisiting the *Society of the Spectacle* in the post-9/11 world. *CONTEMPORARY issues 4*(1): 18–28.

Rose M (2017). *Women walking Manchester: desire lines through the 'original modern' city*. Sheffield: University of Sheffield.

Rogers CE, Farson RE (1957). *Active Listening*. Chicago, IL: University of Chicago Industrial Relations Center.

# 3 | Room to breathe
## Chris Powell

I have always loved walking, whether alone or, more often, in company, and I have always loved escaping outdoors. Aged four, I was found on my bicycle, with a gang of accomplices, heading along the unfinished, empty M4 being built beside my home in South Wales. There was an excitement about setting out into the unknown, without any idea of our destination.

With hindsight and psychoanalytic perspective, I now think that the excitement of setting out without knowing where I would end was partly what made me a group analyst. I wonder if we sought only adventure, or whether there was also unconscious protest at the intrusion of the monolithic concrete flyover, towering over our play space.

My urge to be outside is still powerful. At night, the desire for a warm, comfortable bed is equally strong, so I've never been a camper, nor an early riser. But, by lunchtime, I'll gladly be on the hills. I grew up in South Wales, with sea to the south and west and hills to the north and east. The English Midlands, where I spent my 20s, were dry and flat, so I would flee to the Peak District. Yorkshire, where I settled in my 40s, with land rising up around me, felt more familiar. I miss the sea, but the Dales have their pleasures and rivers.

All these are not pure experiences of the outdoors; all are enlarged by people encountered, even in remote places. Places matter, but people make my memory. I recall hillwalking above Todmorden, along causeys – ancient paved pathways. We were following a route from a book written to promote development in Todmorden after years of economic destruction. The walk and landscape were splendid, but what sticks in my mind is our encounter with a lone walker. We stopped, talked, and discovered he was the book's author. The day and place became alive with his anger at Thatcher's government, and his determination to bring visitors and money into the area. We left his company invigorated.

This chapter is a reflection on a series of walks I and a colleague have created and conducted, four times each year since 2006, in the company of strangers, colleagues and friends, always knowing the route but never knowing where it would take us. It also explains the inspirations for these walks and their roots in applied group analysis, and suggests their connections with psychogeography.

## Room to Breathe

In 2005, I approached a friend and colleague, Andrew Wilson, with an idea. I wanted to create a series of walking days for professional development for people working in mental health. I approached Andrew because he is a close friend with a keen understanding of people. I liked that, where I saw a hill walk, he saw a race track; where I saw a destination pub, he saw a pit-stop. When we first met, through mutual close friends, I liked him straight away but realised that, if we were to share the outdoors, I'd have to slow him down and limit him to respectable distances. These planned walks seemed the ideal way. In addition, I valued the reassurance of a co-conductor who was a competent doctor, for medical emergencies, and also a marathon runner capable of fetching help.

We started the walks, which we called Room to Breathe, in spring 2006, as part of my work running the Tuke Centre at The Retreat psychiatric hospital in York. We continued the walks when I left The Retreat to set up in independent practice as a group analyst and organisational consultant. Since then, the group has continued, with a changing membership, in the original format of four seasonal walks each year, with a group analytic ethos.

We planned the first group to meet four times through 2006, in spring, summer, autumn and winter, and to follow the same route each time, to experience the impact on our walking and talking of the passing of time and changing of the seasons. The first year, we walked eight miles across Nidderdale moorland. The group met at 9.30am, we gave each of the six participants an identical camping chair to carry, and we set off. We stopped half-way, at the highest point, and ate our packed lunches. This was followed by an hour's group analytic conversation, sitting in a circle on our camping chairs. Having tried it out first, Andrew and I decided 60 minutes would be more bearable and safer than the usual group-analytic 90 minutes: in midwinter, on top of a Yorkshire moor, it was cold – very, very cold. At the end of the hour, we continued the circular walk to finish where we began, at 4pm.

Some of the six participants were strangers to each other; others knew two or three people. The membership was closed, with everyone committing themselves to attend all four days through the year. Everyone attended the first three groups but three were absent, with apologies, from the final group.

The group worked well enough. I was surprised by how similar it was to the indoor groups I led. There was a preoccupation with group boundaries in the early stages, then a shift towards personal sharing and exploring experience and learning. Everyone who joined this first group said they enjoyed it, alongside complaints about the weight of the chairs, the weather, our leadership and all else. Those who completed all four walks were satisfied with the experience and described a variety of learning and change. Shared themes included journeying, belonging, ageing and retirement, alongside individual preoccupations. We understood that the reasons why some did not complete all four walks were to do with the group's physical and psychological challenges.

We were able to apply group analytic methodology. We attended to the life of the group, its communication and relationships, its unconscious processes and its development. We addressed the group and its individuals. Working in a group analytic fashion was impeded much less than expected by the unboundaried physical setting.

Having enjoyed this venture, Andrew and I decided to repeat it, but to move it to another location, in the Dales. We added a short group conversation at the start and end, for initial introductions, and a closing reflection on the day, to help contain the group. We also chose a route with a more varied landscape.

We had picked the shooting moors for the first walk because of the relatively blank canvas they present, akin to the presence of the psychoanalyst as a 'blank screen'. However, we discovered that, combined with prevailing British overcast weather (like being inside a Tupperware box, as Bill Bryson puts it), it made the four walks too similar and lacked a sense of the changing seasons. We also decided to increase the size of the group to a maximum of 12 people, plus the two of us, as the greatest number that could easily hear each other talk in a circle on top of a hill.

Since 2006, the walks have continued and developed but always within the overall structure of meeting four times a year, once in each season, and starting, pausing in the middle and ending sat in a circle to talk in group analytic fashion. We have had to cancel once because of the weather and once because of a family emergency, and we once returned by the same route from the starting place because of treacherous conditions. In 12 years (at the time of writing), we have completed 46 walks, each one starting and ending in the same place but arriving somewhere psychologically different.

We set out to provide an opportunity for people to walk and talk in the open air. This much we achieved. We also intended that people might have some of the benefits of structured talking, built on a group analytic model with the additions of the external environment, changing seasons and physical activity. These, we hoped, would add dimensions that were absent indoors.

## Walking and talking

I worked in organisational development before psychotherapy and frequently used walking exercises. In particular, I used a practice called the Emmaus walk. This is based on the biblical story: two men are transformed by walking and talking with a stranger, whom they realise later is the resurrected Christ. A Franciscan friend, Brother Ramon, introduced me to a model of reflection based on this: two people set out and talk something over between them. After 30 minutes, they stop, then retrace their steps back in silence. I used this with clients and was always struck by the richness discovered through discussion on the way out, combined with silent reflection returning.

I also realise that many of the most telling conversations of my life have been with my partner or friends while hillwalking. Sometimes these have been spontaneous conversations, sometimes deliberate attempts to address milestones: relationships, careers, children. Walking and talking always helped; something always changed.

I wonder what makes talking while walking different to conversations over a meal, in a lounge, or in a therapy room. I think five factors particularly contribute to our saying things while walking that we might not say otherwise.

## 1. Physical effort

Even mild physical exertion creates change in our bodies with the potential to impact our emotional state. The breathing of outdoor air, the temperature on our skin, the increased movement of blood in the veins all cause a change in our internal states. Hormones and neurotransmitters are stimulated and change when we move.

## 2. Shared endeavour

Going through something together can build confidence and trust in the other. Although psychotherapists like to think we go through therapy with our clients, and often experience it as challenging, that is not always evident to the other person in the room. There is no room for doubt when you both complete a walk together.

## 3. Environmental impact

As with physical exertion, the external environment also has an impact on mood and emotion at biological and psychological levels. The stimulation of what comes into view – sky, trees, fields, distant towers – and into physical contact – cold, wet, nettles, sunshine – affects our thinking.

## 4. Duration

I often walk round my local park for 30 minutes. When I set out on a walk with family or friends, though, it's usually for a few hours, and often a whole day. There is much to be said for swift exchanges, the discipline of time-limited therapies, and the achievements conjured by deadlines. However, some thoughts and words take time to emerge. Walking allows more time in another's presence than is often possible or tolerable indoors.

## 5. Not facing each other

People walk side by side, occasionally one behind the other on narrow paths, but never face to face. It can be freeing not to look at another or feel their gaze. Direct gaze is used by many therapists for support and challenge. However, in my individual psychotherapy, I place the chairs at an angle, not face-on, to allow the possibility of looking into space, not always at the other. In the group work, we do face each other but in a circle, so that no one is under constant watch and there are plenty of places to look. Walking allows a freedom to look where we will and not feel scrutinised. The environment of the walk affects the micro-geography of the exchange.

Ralph Stacey (2003) theorises the impact of talking in his book *Complexity and Group Process*. He uses complexity theory as a paradigm for change, drawing on Elias's (2000) notion that all we know about people is that they are bodies, in the same way that all matter is a body of one sort or other. Complexity theory proposes that any two bodies in proximity exert an influence on each other, whether at the scale of planets or tiny atoms. Stacey argues we can think of people similarly: we cannot encounter another without change occurring. Moreover, the nature of this change is highly complex and what appears random may in fact be organised in complex ways. His belief is that conversations likewise create change in ways that are unpredictable and cannot always be controlled.

I suggest that walking with others outdoors provides added stimulation to that potential for change. It also connects with the idea that learning happens at points of disequilibrium, when unexpected things are seen, felt and stumbled over. As a psychotherapist, walking seems counter-cultural to my training but simultaneously too powerful a tool to neglect. Moreover, my experience as a group analyst tells me that whatever is gained by walking with another is amplified and deepened when walking with a group.

## Group analysis – the underpinning

Group analysis was created by SH Foulkes, a German-born psychiatrist and psychoanalyst of Jewish descent who emigrated to Britain in 1933. He had encountered Gestalt psychology when working with Kurt Goldstein and was influenced by the sociological and anthropological thinking of the Frankfurt School. He was particularly influenced by his friendship with the sociologist Norbert Elias and his ideas about the primary social nature of people, the need to belong, and the significance of transpersonal and cultural influences. All this formed Foulkes' model of group therapy, group analysis, now used widely around the world and still a pre-eminent model for group therapy in the NHS.

Specific aspects of group analysis make Room to Breathe distinctive and provide a connection with psychogeography.

### 1. Free-floating discussion

Foulkes (1948) insisted that his groups should have no agenda and should not encourage people to take turns or place any constraint on what was said. Rather, in a development from Freud's concept of free association, he encouraged people to say what they were thinking and feeling, particularly in response to the present experience of the group. This can be trickier to achieve than it perhaps seems but, when it occurs, this free-floating discussion allows access to unconscious processes within individuals and the group as a whole. In relation to Room to Breathe, it means we don't offer guidance to the group on what to talk about, either as we walk or when we sit for our group in the middle of the day. We simply ask everyone to introduce themselves at the start of the day, and have a period of reflection at the end, to provide a framework within which we encourage spontaneous exchange.

### 2. Expertise of the group

Foulkes (1975) defined group analysis as 'a form of psychotherapy by the group, of the group, including its conductor'. In practice this means that members of an analytic group become each other's therapists, often displaying greater empathy and insight towards a fellow member than is available to me, as a professional. In Room to Breathe, Andrew and I talk with group members, but primarily they help each other by listening, questioning, commenting, sometimes challenging or even advising. Our main role is administrating the walk, making sure everyone starts together and returns safely. Beyond that, our contribution is no more or less valid than everyone else's, even though our position seems to lend us undue authority.

### 3. Belonging as change

Foulkes saw individuals as primarily healthy, with their struggles or mental health problems a small part of what they bring to a group. He saw the group as providing a healthy, collective whole that could support individuals' particular deficits. To do this, the individuals need to develop a network of communication that enables them to feel part of the group, so they can then be shaped by their group membership. In this aspect, group analysis is curiously congruent with behaviourism, where the stimulus and response of group members is a significant vehicle for therapeutic change. Foulkes (1964) called this 'ego training in action'.

Within Room to Breathe, there is an exchange as people swap experience, knowledge and insight. They normalise each other's struggles and anxieties and offer each other hope for change and resolution. Some participants join us for just one walk, but those who attend over time start to experience the changing of the seasons and the development of a sense of belonging, and something in them starts to shift.

### 4. Sitting in a circle

The heart of Room to Breathe is in the middle of the day, when we sit in a circle, on camping stools, and talk for an hour. We don't have the circular table that occupies the centre of analytic groups, but otherwise we follow the group analytic practice of identical chairs set in the same environment each time.

### 5. Differences

Although Room to Breathe is an application of group analytic methods, it differs from group analysis in a number of key ways.

All members of an analytic group are strangers, with no contact outside group sessions. Our participants often have professional or personal connections outside the group, although some join us because it is distinct from their everyday relationships.

We also routinely fall into sub-groups as we walk, usually twos and threes. This means some things are talked about between some participants but not known by all. In group analysis, all communication is kept within the whole group and any contact outside the group is brought back into it.

The introduction and reflection at the start and end of the day are also not features of group analysis, and nor is the degree of participation and self-disclosure that Andrew and I use.

## Relationship with psychogeography

I have only recently encountered psychogeography, and Room to Breathe does not conform to some of its expectations, as I understand them. We walk a prescribed route, we do not 'drift'; we deliberately inhabit a rural environment, leaving the urban behind. However, Coverley (2010: 96) asserts that the *dérive* 'may lack a clear destination but it is not without purpose'. So, although our walk is more geographically structured than a psychogeographical wandering, it shares intentionality. In Debord's (1967/1992) case, the purpose of the walk is to interrogate the urban environment; in ours, it is to explore the participants' worlds.

There are other points of contact. Chris Rose (2016) provides a succinct definition of two key elements in psychogeography:

> Psychogeography is concerned with the effect of geographical location upon emotion and behaviour; this is tied to an emphasis upon walking, paying critical attention to the (generally but not exclusively) urban landscape and the power structures that have shaped it.

Certainly, we intend that the location and environment of the group will have an effect on emotions and behaviour. Also, although our landscape is rural, it is nonetheless constructed, which leads to socio-political reflection. The landscape invites discussion of ownership, shooting, access, animal rights and climate change. There is frequently a thematic connection with participants' experiences of employment in bureaucratised organisations working to politicised agendas, their experiences of power dynamics in personal and professional relationships and the impact of economics, employment and society on those relationships.

Although our physical route is predetermined, our conversations, thoughts and feelings are allowed to float freely where they will – to drift. This provides some equivalence with Debord's *dérive* (1967/1992).

So, our *dérive* is intersubjective and internal in what we talk about and where our thoughts and feelings lead. There is encouragement to notice what is thought and felt in response to each other and to use that to talk further.

As explained above, we do encourage people to introduce themselves and the preoccupations they bring at the start of the walk. However, this is solely to provide a psychological starting point, a place of departure, rather than to set any agenda. People are free to talk about these preoccupations during the day, but we find that, inevitably, their conversation with others takes them to places they had not anticipated.

## The experience of the group

In 2017, we added a fifth walk into our year. This walk, around Grassington in May, was limited to people who had attended any of the groups previously. Most of the eight participants who joined us had attended three or four times each year for several years. We returned to a previous route with beautiful environmental and geographical variety. As Andrew put it: 'Churchyard, high street, cobbles, clints and grikes, sheep, limekilns, farmers, mill-run, woodland, rivers and cow dung – this walk has it all.'

The purpose of this walk was to provide data for this chapter from participants' first-hand accounts. At the start and end of the day, I asked questions about their experience of the group and the environment. These conversations were recorded and transcribed. Participants also made notes on postcards for me before talking at the start and end, and sent me another postcard some time later, with further reflections.

The rest of the day ran according to the usual pattern.

To start, individuals wrote their response to the question: 'What is it like being here?' Their postcards recorded excitement, anticipation, nervousness, a host of sensory inputs (the river beside us, birds, wind, flowers, and warmth, and also a sense of finding bearings, settling, being connected and being open). Their thoughts communicated a sense of being open and ready, of expanding into the space around us.

There was some self-consciousness:

> The bizarre nature of this group must look even more bizarre for onlookers when we are all sat here writing postcards. Perhaps we look like Victorian landscape painters.

We then spoke. Here are some verbatim extracts:

> I like coming completely away from where I live.

> There is something about the kind of intentional opportunity of doing this, and… I am anticipating. There is an Ignatian idea about allowing your inner compass to settle, so I'm expecting that to happen to some extent during the day.

> I have a sense of not wanting to pre-empt what will emerge quite naturally on the way, so I'm more into process. That's what I'm looking forward to, what emerges.

> I don't know how this route unfolds. But the route for me provides a kind of framework, or space within which the ideas and conversations can unfold… and be sort of held within that.

> I was quite excited by the weather forecast, that we might have lots of dramatic weather.

> Settling, not settled, but settling. But that makes me how you described, that there'll be a settling of my inner compass

today. Curious. And the other word is exposed. I think there
is something about not being near a shelter, and about not
knowing what I or you are going to talk about.

I was thinking about the people as... individual signs in some
way. But what strikes me now as I listen... we almost all come
to point in the same direction as the day goes by, which has
something of the compass.

I think that's a beautiful idea. I'm thinking of the very cheap
compasses I had as a boy. If you wobbled them at all they went
all over the place. You have to put them very still on a table
for them to actually find north. And I was thinking about the
distractions, all the forces at work in a city, unsettling, making
a compass spin. Maybe in some small ways our individual
compasses might fall into place in this environment. But does
that mean they all face the same direction, do we all find north or
do we just find our own individual north? There is something in
what other people say that starts to resonate with you.

There will be discrimination in what everyone goes away with,
but fundamentally there is something common that is touched.

In their words at the start, I heard themes about settling, emerging,
unfolding, the unknown in the place and each other, curiosity,
exposure, alignment and resonance. There was a dynamic between
security and discovery, comfort and adventure.

The day unfolded as these days do: walking, talking, pausing,
configuring and reconfiguring into twos and threes as we went. At
lunchtime we sat in our circle on an old lime kiln, as our ancestors
might have gathered around a fire. We had no fire, but we did
have sandwiches, cakes, stories and conversation.

One distinctive feature of this day was the weather. Despite
our seeking out routes that are more responsive to the changing
seasons, there is often a similarity between our walks. This day,
though, had everything: baking sun, freezing rain, wind, cloud,
cold and even, at the end, crow-black clouds, chuntering thunder
and, finally, spears of lightning. We sat in a circle by the river,

where we began, and I invited participants to note on their postcards, 'What's it like being here?' People wrote of being damp, sweaty, more connected, elated, at peace, relaxed, relieved, joyous and centred by the Dales and the sheep; they wrote about voices, laughter, rain, of being grateful, tired and connected with the land.

Then I again invited the group to talk, this time about 'Being here now', as the black clouds began to roll in. These are again the edited verbatim extracts of our conversation. It spontaneously began by focusing on connections between the people present and the walk as a metaphor for life.

> I came as an individual with… some sense of relationship but I feel… a bit more connected.

> I've had some really interesting conversations that have made me think in different ways… And those sparks have made me think about moving on…

> I think there is something about the process that makes your brain unwind… about life is hard, and maybe it's how you react. Almost like, how do you react to the weather? Well… we put a coat on and keep ourselves warm. So, how do you react to the things that go on in your life? Sometimes it's that unwinding of your brain that gives you a little bit of space to actually look at it rather than react to it.

> I always feel at the end of the walks… how important it is to be in the space now, because of the journey. The journey is a way of… checking in to what we are really attuned to… the outside, nature, sounds, smells, atmospheres, exchanges. All those things are really very easily suppressed or forgotten.

> I was really struck… when we were talking about walking being a very primal activity and something very central to evolutionary biology… primitive.

> I've been reading about Aboriginal songlines… because they believe that creation was sung into being. They walk along the

songlines while remembering how that happened. I think that's almost part of it, being grounded in the world.

I've enjoyed starting and ending by the river… there is a lot of movement going on in there, where we are here. All the different stories within all the different chapters of the walk.

I also really like that the weather's really changeable... we've finally got some dramatic black sky… Being… in the countryside in dramatic weather helps me to feel stuff. The changeability of the weather makes me think, because I go through dark phases, there's always a pattern to things, there's always a cycle, and you have big, black, dramatic clouds but they pass from you. I quite like seeing that.

I'm not quite sure in what way today has been affirming but it's a different satisfactory sense than I would have had, had I walked it on my own. I think it links to the little bits of conversations you drop in and out of or you weave in and out of throughout the day, that speak to you, or that particularly resonate. Something about the way they string together. String together like your necklace.

It's made me go back to everyone being like a signpost here. It's almost like each person has offered something small and precious which [like] a signpost is helping me along.

That's why I feel excited, because it's not an arrow. It's not the way I'm going to follow now. It's more like lots of snippets everybody has contributed that make me feel I can look again at where life is going. So, there are connections with things that have already happened in life, but it's more exciting. It's not just recognition.

The conversation then moved on to the place itself.

I can remember conversations I had three or four years ago, on the walk, and when I came to the place, I remembered the conversations I'd had… Almost like when different music reminds you of different places or different things.

It feels a well-walked series of paths. So, there's a kind of depth to the grooves… that my feet, our feet, are contributing to and our stories are layering on top of that.

I think the place is welcoming; I like it bearing the traces of its human agricultural history. All those stone walls… the horse, and the sheep.

There's an interesting sense what we talk about sits into… this bigger context of paths that have been walked over ages. There becomes something of scale… that my questions are more transitory than some of the stuff we've walked through. So, that adds a helpful sense of perspective.

If we did this in an urban environment, you don't make a mark on a pavement do you? It doesn't change. Whereas you can't walk across a field without compressing the soil and the grass, and cumulatively you become part of creating a route, creating a path, maintaining a path. Whereas concrete will be there, regardless of who walks on it.

You also don't see the evidence of other path-goers, do you, in a city, in quite the same way? That's what is important, I think, to me about the pathways.

It's the ancient, ancient history, following the glacier, that were everywhere in this part of the world. I just feel I could almost be pushing that glacier along because I'm part of the same history.

I was running with a friend of mine, on Ilkley Moor. It was getting dark and we were running this old, old path, and I know it's over a thousand years old, this particular route. And I remembered watching *Roots* on the telly the first time it was on, and there's a scene in it where his forbearers are running along a path that he's walking along… When I walk around here, I get that sense of the paths being trodden for centuries, a sense of what has been before. Bits of it feel very fresh and new… but other bits are old ways.

I think the place that we were having our lunch, that sort of landscape, is what I love best, where it's just so open… I often have to go places because I feel trapped. You have to go somewhere where there is a wide-open space you can see.

It was the place that we remembered that the sky was big.

Yes, because… it starts to impinge on the real horizon. It's kind of at eye level; you haven't got to lift your head to see the sky.

I just want to put a word in for the beautiful walls. There's a lot of hard graft in those walls, there's a lot of man hours, and it would be men, right, as we said? But, interestingly, having made the observations about the paths and previous people… the bit of the landscape that I remember particularly today was walking through the gorge, following where the water had furrowed the stone over the years and made those beautiful, smooth channels. I just really enjoyed following the course of the river in its absence. There's a certain awe in that, somehow, because it must have passed through there fast and hard, you know, to wear that away. A ghostly fast and furious presence is sort of there but it's quite safe to walk there today because it's so dry. It's also extremely beautiful. Something also about following in the footsteps of, er… I don't know what a river's footsteps would be called. Flow? Flow channels?… I think I was more flowy in myself in that gorge.

The water exerted incredible force, but it did it over such a long time, so there's this power and patience beyond anything that I could comprehend in myself in terms of patience. It's not like it was just going to gouge through overnight. And that contrasts to me with some cityscapes that have appeared in my lifetime. So, it reminds me that sometimes the furrow that I'm contributing to, the beauty of it may not be seen until long after I'm gone and others have trod the same path.

I'm trying to formulate some ideas about the gorge and the
smoothness and shininess of the rocks and how they've been
formed like that because of the very harsh and forceful, wild
nature of other rocks rubbing against them, as well as the water.
We are always talking in metaphors; it just feels like that's what
happens – you go through lots of difficult times and the world
treats you badly, or you feel like you've been treated badly, but
the outcome is a smoothness and a furrow that's clear.

We were talking at one point about that whole cycle… and how
it's reassuring that you know, whatever happens, here's spring
again. It's that remembering and that reassurance of the whole
year; that no matter whatever happens, spring comes round… I
like that on the walk, the whole cycle of the year.

I was struck that the second conversation had become more primal
in its connection to history, open spaces and long timespans. I
also noted that, of all the features of the walk, including a village,
fields, farms, moors, hills and trees, the one that attracted most
comment was a deep gorge we had scrambled down. It was the
most confined, difficult and potentially dangerous section of the
walk, even on a dry day.

The conversation ended just as the thunder and lightning
overtook us and we made our way back to our cars as heavy drops
of rain fell around us.

## Postscript

I had invited people to write another postcard and send it to me in
the weeks following this walk. These are some of their comments.

The physical geography… facilitates reflection and conversation
– particularly conversations which might be difficult in a 'sterile'
face-to-face context. There is something about the rhythm, the
effort of movement over the landscape, which encourages a
process of movement through ideas and reflections.

The rural environment doesn't talk 'at' you; to explore the
outdoors one must engage faculties beyond language. And so, as

the day unfolds and the landscape moves through us, we cease our need to advertise who and what we are and we turn instead to being together in the most natural, human way.

A few weeks later, the sense of things settling remains and is part of the draw of participating in the walk. Recent weeks have been troubled in our country. Sitting together with those things that trouble us just seems important.

Movement physically and in the environment somehow embodies the possibility of change and movement towards change.

'The path as the frame': the ebb and flow, the receding and the unfolding, conversations with the shared walking of a path.

## Some discussion and conclusions

These excerpts illustrate how the external environment, including the weather and the geography and all that populates it, have an impact on the walk and the walkers. This was very explicit on this particular day's walk, but I have noticed that this impact is there, consciously or not, every time we meet. More interesting to me is the level at which this impact is noticed: less at the superficial level of what is seen and more at a visceral, primal level, evoking connections not just between people in the group but with a wider, ancestral humanity. Group analysts think not just of a dynamic matrix of communication between people in the group in the present but also of a foundation matrix, biologically and culturally shared with all of humanity, which allows, demands even, communication and connection in the first place.

This also evokes a resonance between members of the group so their lives and present struggles find a place within some greater story. While specific answers or solutions may still be elusive, a renewed sense of purpose, direction and endurance emerges. The individual preoccupation is shifted onto a larger social and geographical canvas, with wider horizons, broader perspectives and more fundamental meanings.

I suggest the combination of a group analytic structure (including the dynamic administration of the walk) with the external environment creates a form of containment for enriching conversation. I believe this adds a security and efficacy that would be absent without the group analytic framework. In a therapeutic space, the conversation and exploration are contained within a relationship with a therapist or a group. In our open space, this containment is provided by the group's structure and is taken on by the participants through their connections with each other. I think this is what allows us to meet the environment face and flesh on, to survive, and to emerge weathered, worn and renewed through the seasons.

Returning to my M4 excursion as a small child, I think there was an element of protest about it: I was escaping the constraints of my home, setting out towards new horizons. In just this way, I think our seasonal walks in the Dales to talk and think are an act of protest at the constraints of everyday life and work and an acknowledgement of our visceral and psychic need to see the horizon, risk the rain on our heads and place our feet on paths that others have trod before and will tread after us.

## Acknowledgements

Thank you to: Andrew, of course, and to all who walk and talk with us, but especially Cath, Helen, Jane, Jill, Martin, Rowan, Sonia and Sophie. For further information, visit www.spark. uk.net/room-to-breathe

## References

Coverley M (2010). *Psychogeography.* Harpenden: Pocket Essentials.

Debord G (1967/1992). *The Society of the Spectacle.* London: Rebel Press.

Elias N (1939/2000). *The Civilising Process.* Oxford: Blackwell.

Foulkes SH (1975/1986). *Group Analytic Psychotherapy.* London: Karnac.

Foulkes SH (1964/1984). *Therapeutic Group Analysis.* London: Karnac.

Foulkes SH (1948/1983). *Introduction to Group Analytic Psychotherapy.* London: Karnac.

Rose C (2016). *Walking together: psychogeography and psychotherapy.* [Blog.] Sketching, psychotherapy and beyond; 20 December. https://chrisrose.me/2016/12/20/walking-together-psychogeography-and-psychotherapy (accessed 31 March 2019).

Stacey RD (2003). *Complexity and Group Process.* Hove: Brunner-Routledge.

# 4 | Mindfulness in the city: taking notice as therapeutic practice

## Benedict Hoff and Richard Phillips

I'm seated crossed-legged on the floor in a south London living room, leading a four-stage meditation. I ring the bell to signal the end of the meditation and invite the group to slowly get up in silence, move towards the front door and gather on the pavement outside. We space ourselves in a line about five metres apart – I position myself in the middle, allowing a participant to lead the procession. We begin walking, slowly and deliberately, noticing what this most mundane of activities, so frequently done on automatic pilot, actually feels like – the sensations of our feet striking the ground, the movement of our limbs, the rhythm of our breath. Gradually, our gaze rises from our feet and we start taking in the city around us. A dilapidated block of flats with bright strings of washing flapping in the wind meets my eyes, before a cat darts across the road, diverting my attention towards a wall featuring interesting graffiti and the message: 'Real homes for real people.' Suddenly, I'm aware of the aroma of 'churros y chocolate' emerging from a Venezuelan restaurant I've never noticed before, and I feel my stomach rumbling. We're only a couple of blocks from the chaos of the Old Kent Road, but the backstreets are strangely quiet, apart from some parakeets cackling in a nearby tree. I'm vaguely aware of somebody observing us and notice my mind creating a

narrative about what they might be thinking. And yet, somehow,
I don't care. My absorption in the scene unfolding around
me and the sense of connectedness I feel towards my silent
companions is total and utter.

The above vignette describes a scene from one of three Mindfulness in the City workshops that I (Benedict Hoff) led and devised in dialogue with Richard Phillips, the co-author of this paper. These workshops attempted to translate mindfulness practices from the ordered space of the meditation hall or yoga studio to the messier realities of everyday life. They explored three main questions that we address in this chapter:

1.  How can we practise mindfulness in urban settings?
2.  How can we encourage and support others to be mindful in these settings?
3.  What are the benefits of urban mindfulness – of 'taking notice in the city' – in terms of wellbeing?

## Points of departure: therapy, curiosity and psychogeography

I am a trained mindfulness teacher and integrative therapist and Richard is a researcher who is currently working on experiences and applications of curiosity. The workshops emerged from our conversations with each other. Richard's research explores a series of 'spaces for curiosity' in which curiosity is variously tolerated, practised, encouraged and invested in, and had already begun to explore mindfulness in ordinary places (Phillips, Evans & Muirhead, 2015). These range from learning environments in which curiosity may be a driver of independent and effective learning (Phillips & Johns, 2012) to initiatives in which curiosity is endorsed as a pathway to friendship (Phillips & Evans, 2016) and/or to health and wellbeing (Phillips, Evans & Muirhead, 2015). I was particularly interested in a series of undergraduate field trips Richard had led in Liverpool. Here, the students' fieldwork was supported by particular ways of engaging with and taking notice of the urban landscape. These spoke readily to mindfulness, and particularly its practice 'off the cushion', in the form of mindful walking. It was this dialogue between geography fieldwork and mindfulness that interested us and that subsequently informed our design of the Mindfulness in the City workshops.

Richard had previously interviewed Sam Thompson, an author of a report about 'five ways to wellbeing' commissioned by the UK government for its 2008 Foresight report on *Mental Capital and Wellbeing* (Foresight Mental Capital and Wellbeing Project, 2008). The report, produced by the New Economics Foundation (NEF, 2008), advocated a form of mindfulness, badged as 'Take notice', as one of the five recommended keys to mental health. Sam had explained that 'Take notice' translated ideas and practices that some people might find esoteric into others that they might recognise and find more comfortable. Rather than encouraging mindfulness meditation *per se*, 'Take notice' invited people to be curious in their everyday lives:

> Be curious. Catch sight of the beautiful. Remark on the unusual. Notice the changing seasons. Savour the moment, whether you are walking to work, eating lunch or talking to friends. Be aware of the world around you and what you are feeling. (Foresight Mental Capital and Wellbeing Project, 2008: 21)

The five ways to wellbeing have been adopted in public health and wellbeing strategies and projects such as the Liverpool Decade of Health and Wellbeing and endorsed by mental health organisations such as Mind. Richard interviewed some of those in the primary care trust (the local statutory healthcare provider) and mental health services in the Liverpool area that were attempting to implement 'Take notice', along with the other ways to wellbeing ('Connect', 'Be active', 'Keep learning', and 'Give'). His findings revealed mixed feelings about 'Take notice': that it had a lot of potential but that it was difficult to implement (Phillips, Evans & Muirhead, 2015). If it was going to work, 'Take notice' would need investment. This raises practical questions, which we take up in this chapter.

The 'Take notice' initiative involves and encourages a particular quality of attention to everyday geographies. Herein lies a broadly psychogeographical dimension, which begins with disrupting habitual forms of environmental perception and extends to the cultivation of alternative ways of perceiving, apprehending or experiencing the same spaces. This psychogeography reaches beyond some 'usual suspects' who are commonly cited as a kind of shorthand for psychogeography itself – notably, Guy Debord and his fellow Situationists – and draws attention to others who cultivated and demonstrated forms of attention to everyday geographies that resonate with mindfulness practices. These others include Georges Perec. The quality of attention that Perec cultivated, practised and documented in his *lieux* (places) project is, arguably if implicitly, mindful (Phillips, 2016). Thus, when we were developing these field-based mindfulness workshops, we were able to draw on a wealth of geographical and psychogeographical experience and expertise, extending from those such as Perec to more contemporary urban explorers and fieldworkers (Phillips & Johns, 2012).

## Workshops and research methods

We have raised a number of practical questions about how to translate mindfulness from meditation halls and yoga studios to ordinary places – questions about how to take notice in the city. The challenge is to translate, relocate and potentially 'scale up' mindfulness practices without diluting or compromising them. This section explains how a series of Mindfulness in the City workshops were devised and conducted, establishing the context for reflections on the workings of these workshops and the insights gained from them. This experience is not presented as a blueprint for others to follow, but rather as a set of experiences from which to learn.

We have alluded to a difference between formal, guided meditation practice, conducted in 'stable' indoor environments relatively free from external distractions, and 'everyday' mindfulness as it is practised in the messier, less predictable world outside. In the context of mindfulness as it is generally taught, these two aspects of mindfulness practice share a symbiotic relationship, complementing and depending on each other. However, as the principles of mindfulness have been promoted more widely and made more accessible, these two complimentary aspects have sometimes become decoupled – 'mindful running' or 'mindful photography', for example, which do not actually include any formal meditation practice.

To some observers, this initiative might be seen as a compromise, a dilution of mindfulness into the devalued and easy counterpart – 'McMindfulness'. However, mindfulness is compatible with everyday life and speaks readily to contemporary Buddhist practice, particularly recent interpretations of Zen teachings (see, for example, Beck, 1995, 1997). Moreover, the practice of mindfulness in ordinary places is consistent with arguments advanced in contemporary critical health and wellbeing geography that almost any landscape – not simply pastoral landscapes, which previously dominated the literature on therapeutic landscape – can be therapeutic if we learn to engage with it in a particular way (Little, 2012: 218).

In our discussions about what form the workshops would take, I felt that, to translate mindfulness to the everyday without compromise or dilution, it was important that it remained true to its origins in meditative practice. Therefore, rather than treating Mindfulness in the City as an entirely freestanding workshop, we required that participants have some basic training in the skills necessary to 'take notice' that formal meditation practice helps develop.

Our starting position, which underpins the workshops, is that taking notice can be mindful in and of itself. As the participants' self-reporting in the meditation enquiries suggests, this can be greatly supported and enhanced through the prior practice of formal meditation. In turn, taking notice may not only be mindful but may extend and deepen formal meditation practices themselves as we apply the awareness cultivated in the 'laboratory' of the meditation hall, for example, to the world outside.

When planning and running the workshops, we paid particular attention to the questions posed above, reflecting on the consequences of combining formal, indoor-based meditation with outdoor mindfulness practice within the same workshop; the impact of the workshops on participants' relationships with the places in which the workshops were conducted; the impacts of the workshops in terms of participants' wellbeing, and whether these experiences had disrupted, positively or negatively, the participants' experiences of these places.

Participants were recruited from mindfulness courses that I was already running, and from other meditation centres and a counselling agency. They were asked to read an information sheet detailing the scope and aims of the research and what participation would involve and to sign a consent form before being allowed to take part in the workshops. The participants are given pseudonyms in this paper, for ethical reasons.

**Table 1**: Mindfulness in the City workshops and participants

| Name | Biographical outline | Location | Date |
| --- | --- | --- | --- |
| Anne | 35, White British, health trainer/counsellor | Leyton | 20.05.17 |
| Eleanor | 37, White British, social enterprise director | Leyton | 20.05.17 |
| Shelley | 50, White British, health trainer | London Fields | 25.06.17 |
| Catherine | 32, White British, photographer | London Fields | 25.06.17 |
| Matt | 28, White German, communications/marketing | London Fields | 25.06.17 |
| Tara | 36, Chinese, journalist | London Fields | 25.06.17 |
| Emily | 29, White French, start-up worker | London Fields | 25.06.17 |
| Yvette | 56, White British, counsellor | Elephant & Castle/ Burgess Park | 12.08.17 |
| Rick | 37, White British, works in publishing | Elephant & Castle/ Burgess Park | 12.08.17 |
| Anathi | 49, Black British, yoga teacher and author | Elephant & Castle/ Burgess Park | 12.08.17 |
| Sarah | 52, White British, receptionist/ counsellor | Elephant & Castle/ Burgess Park | 12.08.17 |

The sites for the three workshops were selected so that each would be local to, and therefore presumably familiar to, some or all of the participants. This was because 'taking notice' is conceived as an attempt to experience already-familiar places in unfamiliar ways. Since participants lived in and around three parts of north-east and south-east London, we selected Leyton, London Fields and Elephant and Castle/Burgess Park.

Each workshop comprised three key elements:

1. In the first part – **Imagining and Mapping** – I outlined the general format of the workshop before leading a short focusing exercise to help participants explore how they imagined their local neighbourhood. I then invited participants to engage with local maps of the area and decide on a route for a mindful walk through a range of different urban environments.

2. In the second part – **Attuning and Walking** – I led a four-stage preparatory meditation, to move participants from 'doing mode' to 'being mode' and stimulate greater sensory attunement to their moment-by-moment experience before embarking on the walk itself. Participants would either walk together as a group (spaced a few metres apart) or singly, depending on their preference. They would be invited to engage all their five senses and monitor their embodied experience as they traversed the city.

3. In the third part – **Reconvening and Reimagining** – participants were invited to explore their experience through a free-flowing meditation enquiry and then compare their felt experience of place with their original imaginings of the local area from the opening focusing exercise.

All this was monitored and documented through a reflexive diary that I kept and discussed with Richard, and through short, conversational interviews with the participants. I was interested in collecting two types of data. The first related to observations of individual and group interactions and behaviour, which were recorded mainly in field notes and photographs. The second related to the participants' self-reported experiences of the workshops, which were reported through recordings of the 'group meditation enquiries' (comparable to a focus group). These were transcribed and then analysed by both authors. The research was then written up as a joint endeavour, supported and sustained by insights that we each brought from our own respective fields of expertise – in my case, mindfulness, meditation and Buddhist psychology, and in Richard's, cultural geography, psychogeography and geography fieldwork.

## Imagining and mapping

The workshops described here challenge perceptual habits by inviting participants to take notice of that which they would normally take for granted or fail to see. I sought to apply this understanding, from Buddhist psychology, that the human brain naturally inclines towards 'fixing' our immediate reality by taking a view of the world around us (often based on quite limited information) and 'freezing' it in our minds. Zen Buddhist monk Steven Hagen explains:

> What we want, what we need, is not to be confused. We want to understand. We want to *know*. Neatly packaging everything gives us the illusion that we actually *know* something... Once we get the world arranged, we'll feel more comfortable. (1999: 22)

Participants gave a sense of this 'freezing' in the way they recorded and then described what had emerged for them in the opening focusing exercise. While some were initially hesitant (perhaps disarmed by the boxes of crayons and wacky pen sets), generally they set about the task with enthusiasm, absorption and a certain decisiveness in their drawing or writing on the page in front of them. And the vision they articulated was often very clear, giving a sense of 'I know what this area is about and how it makes me feel'. Consider these impressions of Leyton and London Fields articulated by Eleanor and Emily respectively:

> I had like a bird's-eye view and I was going out to different places and then each of those places was conjuring up associations of what that little area means to me. It was really nice to remember the reasons I really like it around here. (Eleanor, Leyton)

> It's like three different worlds in one... It's a very active area. Kingsland Road, there's a lot of movement: people, cars, people walking day and night. During the night, people screaming, drunk people; it's just a very different atmosphere, depending

> on the time of the day, but I love this… all these changes and
> contrasts in this area. (Emily, London Fields)

These generally positive impressions were quickly qualified by descriptions of what were perceived as more negative characteristics of the same areas:

> We've got like pigeons, which make me feel like it's really grotty
> and they hang around the house… around this bridge. But on
> the other side of the bridge, we have like this nature reserve with
> geese and swans… and that made me connect… the depravity
> with the gentrification and I'm seeing like the swans as the
> gentrification of the area and the pigeons as 'We're still here
> mate'. (Eleanor, Leyton)

Eleanor's metaphor of the 'swans versus the pigeons' alludes to the transformation, and in particular the gentrification, that is now well established in all of the sites visited in the course of this exercise: London Fields, Elephant and Castle/Burgess Park and Leyton. These are dynamic urban areas, characterised by diversity and creativity, but increasingly by social dislocation too. Eleanor was not the only participant to refer to the uneasy dimensions of urban experience. Emily spoke of distressed people:

> It's active and there's a lot of movement-induced noise… Drunk
> people, they are screaming like something bad is happening.
> It's dramatic – my flatmate calls them the lost souls of Kingsland
> Road. Because it really feels like they are in distress. (Emily,
> London Fields)

These observations make the important point that taking notice of the city need not mean aestheticising it – reducing it to a superficial plane of beautiful things and changing seasons. Mindfulness in the City can have quite the opposite effect, by highlighting difficult experiences.

These mental maps – structured around opposites and extremes – betray a tendency to imagine the world in terms of easily digestible opposites. Steve Hagen argues that this dualistic thinking is 'the psychological backdrop for our everyday world of chasing after some things and running away from others' (1999: 53). He concludes that we can become rigid in how we relate to the world around us – noticing the obvious, the loud and the intense (and reacting accordingly with clinging or aversion) at the expense of appreciating the more subtle shades in between: those often quite ordinary but sometimes pleasurable aspects of our urban experience.

## Attuning and walking

I sought to apply principles of meditation/mindfulness – practised, for example, in the 'laboratory setting' of the meditation hall – to the messier realities of everyday settings. These principles revolve around the pursuit of the 'right view', which means *seeing* reality for what it is, in the here and now, moment by moment. It is conceived as a form of knowledge based on what we actually experience rather than what we think – sometimes called 'bare attention' or 'naked awareness' in Buddhist psychology. Zen Buddhism understands this form of knowledge in terms of a return to 'beginner's mind':

> The mind of the beginner is empty, free of the habits of the expert, ready to accept, to doubt, and open to all possibilities. It is the kind of mind which can see things as they are. (Baker, 1970: xiv)

Similarly, some neuropsychologists distinguish between the 'narrative mode' (in which we conceptualise the world around us) and the 'experiential mode' (the realm of direct sensory perception) (see, for example, Williams, 2010). I sought to put these principles into practice by devising a four-stage meditation designed to focus the sensory experiences of the participants, to cultivate some form of 'bare attention' and facilitate such a return to 'beginner's mind', encouraging a shift from 'narrative mode' to 'experiential mode'. The meditation resembled the form of an hour glass: taking in sounds around us, feeling the ground beneath us and the sensation of gravity drawing the body into the chair, then exploring the breathing body as a whole, before focusing in with a very close-up lens of awareness to breath sensations, then expanding again to include attention to sounds, thoughts and emotions and transitioning into a state of 'open monitoring', relinquishing any fixed point of attention and allowing whatever entered the field of awareness simply to come and go without discriminating. We then moved silently into the period of mindful exploration itself, without discussion or conversation.

In the enquiry that followed, it seemed that there had been a process of conceptual 'thawing' as the participants recalled the environment they had just explored. Eleanor, for example, after our walk through Wanstead Flats in Leyton, shared that she recorded in her notebook details about the different sorts of trees she had encountered:

> Normally I'd probably be like, oh there are a load of trees... trees all in the same category. But then being there and exploring, every single tree I looked at was different. I was like, it's not just loads of trees, it's like loads of different things. And yeah, like the different qualities of the leaves... some of them are really papery and some of them are really tough; some of them are really shiny.

'Tree', initially frozen as an abstract, intellectual concept, had kaleidoscoped into a diverse set of multi-faceted, textured realities, which Eleanor got to know by seeing them differently – in my terms, 'seeing things as they really are'. Rick, in turn, was struck by the diversity of the local architecture he discovered through his close visual inspection of the built environment in the residential backstreets around Elephant and Castle/Burgess Park, noting the plethora of different architectural styles, the different textures of the concrete and other building materials, as well various decorative details. He was particularly surprised by how his concept of 'tower block' was challenged when he 'really looked':

> I noticed, when I sort of looked more closely, there, but in other places as well, was people's attempts to personalise… the hanging baskets... It might be perceived as ugly or, you know, because it's a concrete block, but actually, within that, there's beauty.

In the opening focusing exercise, Anathi admitted that her impression of Elephant and Castle was largely defined by childhood memories of the area as a 'slum' that was 'noisy and smelly'. Interestingly, it was the part of the mindful walk through arguably the area's noisiest and smelliest street – the Old Kent Road – that stayed with her and she recalled in far more nuanced (and positive) terms:

> I found the smells really rich… I just thought, oh my God [makes a sniffing noise] there are just so many foods… Someone went to all that effort to cook a meal with all those different spices and it was just like… a lovely experience… I walked the same distance from Bermondsey on my way here and I just went [makes a whooshing noise]. And I didn't see anything.

'Noise' also revealed itself as multi-layered in nature – a concept that failed to capture the complexity of the soundscape that filled Anne's ears in the Leyton workshop:

> I could hear footsteps and doors closing. It was getting more and more dense – the number of things. And then, like, how those things, those subjects, split up into their own little bits – footsteps, but then footsteps sound different on different surfaces, so they were like in their own little gang… and then like cars… but cars sound different when they're stopping and when they're starting. And then like people and birds and all the different types of those.

This increased level of granularity in terms of what people noticed, and the fact that this greater sensory attunement to the details of the urban environment occurred not just through sight but through other senses too, would seem broadly consistent with a shift from 'narrative mode' to 'experiential mode'. Dwelling in body sensations, as we did in the preceding meditation, turned down the volume on the conceptual mind, with its hard-wired biases and inaccurate framing of reality, and opened the door to a perceptual way of experiencing the world. This allowed us to get closer to the simple here-and-now reality of things and perceive more accurately the world around us.

Of course, greater sensory attunement to the urban environment is not always experienced in positive terms. Certainly, participants reported moments where they found the urban environment intrusive and unpleasant, particularly at the levels of sound and smell. Yvette, for example, did not share Anathi's positive experience of the 'smellscape' of the Old Kent Road, and admitted that a lot of the time she was holding her breath. She described the pollution as 'an assault on the senses' that was 'smellable and almost tasteable'. She concluded that there was 'nothing positive in the taste realm' on her walk. Eleanor, in turn, reported similar feelings of displeasure at the unpleasant sounds and smells she detected around the local garage in Leyton on the walk back from the duck pond:

> It's quite obvious when you get back to the road... the smell of the traffic... and the garage next door... you're like, the fucking smell of the garage! Which is annoying.

Eleanor understood this intrusiveness in terms having less 'control' over what entered the landscape of her awareness through sound and smell when compared with sight or touch. She explained: 'You're walking and you think, I don't want to smell that, but you can't stop because you've already smelled it... and it's already "in" you then.'

Yet, on a broader level, participants reported a greater tolerance towards and ability to 'be with' these more challenging aspects of their urban experience. Anathi described the noise on the Old Kent Road as an 'onslaught' but 'not a negative onslaught':

> It just felt very rich, very embracing, very accepting, whereas I think normally I sort of think, what's going on? I'll be judging it... in some shape or form... If you have that level of awareness and you take it all in... I'm not sure I know where I'm going with this, but there's something here about, it *is* possible to live at that level... if you have practice... if you do it in a mindful way. Because you're accepting everything, you're allowing it in... it's not getting to you.

Crucial to Anathi's capacity to accept what was happening around her and 'allow it in' seems to be this non-judgemental attitude she refers to. With her conceptual mind in retreat – with its tendency to divide things up into 'pleasant' and 'unpleasant', a tendency that simultaneously drives the compulsion to relate to our experience with clinging or aversion – she was able to soften into her experience. And, arguably, underpinning this non-judgemental attitude is the 'quality of awareness' to which she refers – an awareness that, as her earlier testimony relating to the Old Kent Road's smellscape suggests, inhabited the domain of the perceptual rather than the conceptual.

This link between 'naked awareness' and the capacity to soften into urban experience emerged in other participant enquiries. Catherine, for example, described feeling initially overwhelmed by the traffic around London Fields. But then, when she shifted her awareness to the visual plane and began inspecting the details of the street around her – the trees and an interesting building façade and how it was framed by the sky – she described a transformation in her experience, which suddenly became 'really peaceful, weirdly'. Yvette, in turn, described feeling 'more connected in general' to the urban environment around Elephant and Castle/Burgess Park after our period of mindful exploration. She contrasted this way of being with how she might 'barricade myself off from the here and now' when normally out and about in London. She attributed this to being 'more in touch with my feelings' and 'my body feeling… out of its habitual way of responding'.

Concurrent with this conceptual thawing of the participants' impressions of the city, the higher degree of granularity in what they noticed, as well as the increased sensory attunement to and capacity to be with (un)pleasant aspects of urban experience, there also emerged a shift towards an apparently more 'approach-orientated' mode of being.

Mindfulness practices apply theories of motivation, taking inspiration in particular from the behavioural-inhibition or avoidance system (BIS) and a behavioural-activation or approach system (BAS). The approach system (correlated with left prefrontal cortex activation) is reward-orientated and associated with positive emotions, including the anticipation of good events. It helps us move towards things that might be good for us. Conversely, the avoidance system (correlated with the right prefrontal cortex) is said to help us avoid things that might threaten us and is associated with more negative emotions such as fear, disgust and repulsion (see, for example, Gray, 1981).

Both avoidance and approach are seen as essential to our wellbeing and survival, but neuroscientists such as Rick Hanson (2014) have suggested that the human brain possesses an inherent 'negativity bias'. He describes the human brain as 'velcro for negative experience but Teflon for positive experience' (2014: 52). He makes the point, however, that this tendency can be compensated for by making the deliberate decision to 'take notice' of both our inner landscape and the world around us. Becoming more aware of all aspects of our experience, he writes, endows us with a greater sense of integration, of inner wholeness. This gives us choice and enables us to 'turn up the volume' on the more pleasant parts of that experience, particularly in the realm of sense perception, and embed them within our implicit memory (2014: 200).

The possibility of learning to counter the negativity bias might help explain the predominance of pleasant and positive details reported by participants when recalling their experience of the mindful walk. These reports pointed towards a concurrent shift towards a more approach-orientated way of being. This manifested in a stronger impulse to reach towards objects within their field of awarenesss. Matt, for example, recalled his interaction with the produce of the fruit and vegetable patch in Dalston Eastern Curve Garden (near London Fields):

> I would have tried a few things that I otherwise would not have tried if I'd just walked into the garden and just sat down. For example, I tried some raspberries and I was wondering, are they actually raspberries or am I just poisoning myself? But then I thought no, these are raspberries. So that was going on and was interesting. I tasted some basil, which I also liked.

Yvette, in turn, reflected on the transition from the Old Kent Road, where she'd described a more avoidance-orientated way of being in relation to the traffic pollution. She recalled that, on arriving at Burgess Park and noticing a patch of wild flowers, she suddenly remembered: 'I could participate and I could actually smell the flowers and I could actually touch them, and I felt that woke up that sense that had been hitherto dormant.'

Feeling curious and 'reaching out' also incorporated a social dimension, with participants reporting a greater sense of social connectedness with the people with whom they were sharing these surroundings. Eleanor, for example, in the Leyton workshop, noticed her displeasure at the 'horrible block of flats' that dominated the horizon on the otherwise green and leafy Wanstead Flats. However, on approaching the rear of the building and taking care to really *sense* the building – noticing the sounds of its inhabitants as well as its visual aspects – her experience shifted:

> I was really struck by those contrasts: those really nice oases of calm and then you've got like… the Flats and I'd never been behind them before. And I felt really like… and I had a real sense of being behind the scenes… I was really aware of that…. that sense of belonging in a place and who else occupied that place.

Rick, in turn, noticed his feeling of 'acceptance' and a shared sense of humanity as he observed strangers socialising in Burgess Park:

> I also really noticed the people around and how, for example in the park, there were people having a BBQ and people playing football, and… a small child who was crying, who ran to her father. And I think what I became conscious of is of all these lives playing out around us and it's so easy to miss those… I felt a real kind of acceptance of all that stuff happening. A kind of noticing of that, and an acceptance of humanity playing out.

Although often practised in a group setting, meditation is nevertheless sometimes caricatured as an introspective activity. In fact, the *metta bhavana* or loving kindness meditation, one of the two foundational cornerstones of meditative practice in Mahayana Buddhism (the other being mindfulness of breathing), is outward facing in nature. Loving kindness meditations appear in various adapted forms in secular mindfulness courses. The Mindfulness in the City workshops allowed participants to broaden this experience to encompass people on the streets around them, with whom they shared no relationship but towards whom they nevertheless experienced a sense of connectedness.

## Reconvening and reimagining: towards a conclusion

This chapter has explored practical questions about how to translate mindfulness practices from ordered indoor spaces dedicated to meditation to ordinary outdoor places. To do this without compromising or diluting them, the workshops remained true to the origins of mindfulness in formal meditative practice. The inclusion of formal meditation practice before, and in some cases during, the mindful walk encouraged a greater shift from 'doing mode' to 'being mode' and stimulated greater sensory attunement to the participants' moment-by-moment urban experience. Without exception, participants reported that they felt that this facilitated the path to wellbeing described above and enhanced their experience of the mindful walk itself. Anne (Leyton) remarked, in relation to the initial four-stage meditation, that it took her 'out of my head' and that she realised:

> I'm really, really not in my body a lot of the time. And I feel like it [the meditation] maybe slows me down a bit, because I would have been like, right, look at this, look at that, touch this, touch that… like, calm down! Umm… yeah, I think it just, I dunno, hones you in more.

Emily (London Fields) similarly felt that formal meditation 'reconnected' her with her senses:

> The full awareness thing, kind of resonated with me today because we were outside and all the senses were stimulated… it helped me connect with this.

Yvette, in turn, associated formal meditation with an intention 'to be in the moment at any given time' during the walk, which she cited as a 'continuation… extension of what we practised in here [the house where the workshop began]'. She concluded that 'my experience would have been very different, much less involved and self-aware if we hadn't had that preparation. I think it was essential'.

More specifically, this chapter has developed an understanding of how this 'taking notice' emerged as a way to wellbeing in the workshops. The more highly attuned form of sensory perception that formal meditation helped participants cultivate prior to the mindful walk enhanced their ability to notice the subtler details of their urban experience that they otherwise would have missed. It also supported their ability to 'be with' more challenging aspects of their experience, which in turn encouraged a shift towards a more approach-orientated way of relating to the city. In these respects, the chapter speaks to broader debates about, and interrogations of, therapeutic landscapes. These are increasingly viewed not as exceptional spaces, physically or psychologically distant from 'normal life', but rather in terms of more 'everyday spaces of care and wellbeing' (Little, 2012: 218).

Nevertheless, this perspective still betrays an implicit understanding of wellbeing as largely dependent on external conditions, whether these relate to a forest retreat or an inner-city care home. Buddhist psychology argues that it is our attachment to this idea that is at the root of our suffering, because it drives our habitual desire to get somewhere – physically, emotionally, spiritually – other than where we actually are, in the often-misguided belief that this will make us feel better. Participant experience during these workshops attests to the fact that it is not necessarily the nature of places in and of themselves that encourages (or not) 'wellbeing'; rather, it is the way in which we relate to them and the manner in which that relationship is mediated.

In this sense, although almost any landscape can be experienced in a way that may benefit wellbeing, and may therefore be a therapeutic landscape, urban mindfulness does not and need not aestheticise the city. The quality of attention to the city that mindfulness cultivates may also heighten awareness of issues such as gentrification and the distress of others and oneself, which may provoke well-justified anger, rather than simply pacify the observer. But only by being aware of such 'negative experience' and noticing our tendency to react to it with resistance or aversion do we give ourselves the choice to respond more creatively to the challenges of city living in ways that might benefit not only our own wellbeing but that of our fellow urban denizens too.

# References

Baker R (1970). Introduction. In: Suzuki S. *Zen Mind, Beginners Mind*. New York, NY: Weatherhill (ppxxi–xx).

Beck CJ (1997). *Everyday Zen*. London: Thorsons.

Beck CJ (1995). *Nothing Special: living Zen*. New York, NY: HarperCollins.

Foresight Mental Capital and Wellbeing Project (2008). *Mental Capital and Wellbeing: Making the Most of Ourselves in the 21st Century*. Final project report. London: Government Office for Science.

Gray JA (1981). A critique of Eysenck's theory of personality. In: Eysenck HJ (ed). *A Model for Personality*. Berlin: Springer-Verlag (pp246–276).

Hagen S (1999). *Buddhism Plain and Simple*. London: Penguin Books.

Hanson R (2014). *Hardwiring Happiness: how to reshape your brain – and your life*. London: Penguin Books.

Little J (2012). The new therapeutic spaces of the spa. In: Atkinson S, Fuller S, Painter J (eds). *Wellbeing and Place*. Farnham: Ashgate (pp 217–230).

New Economics Foundation (2008). *Five Ways to Wellbeing*. London: NEF. www.gov.uk/government/publications/five-ways-to-mental-wellbeing (accessed 14 April 2019).

Phillips R (2016). Georges Perec's experimental fieldwork; Perecquian fieldwork. *Social & Cultural Geography 19*(2): 171–191.

Phillips R, Evans B (2016). Friendship, curiosity and the city: dementia friends and memory walks in Liverpool. *Urban Studies 55*(3): 639–654.

Phillips R, Evans B, Muirhead S (2015). Curiosity, place and wellbeing: encouraging place-specific curiosity as a 'way to wellbeing'. *Environment and Planning A 47*(11): 2339–2354.

Phillips R, Johns J (2012). *Fieldwork for Human Geography*. London: Sage.

Williams M (2010). Mindfulness and psychological process. *Emotion 10*(1): 1–7.

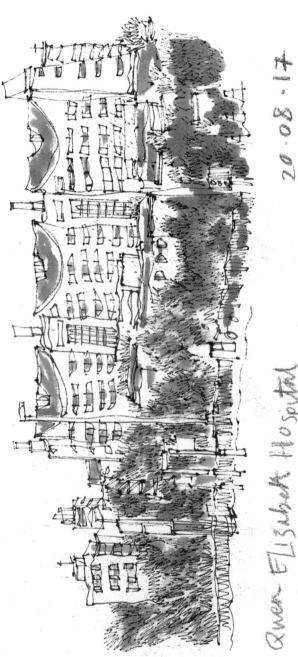

Queen ELizabeth Hospital

20·08·17

# 5 Feeling my way: on walking, embodiment and practising psychotherapy

## Liz Bondi

In the late afternoon, I leave my office, walking along the corridor, down the stairs and out onto the street. Within a few minutes, I am crossing wide, open parkland, following a path bordered by cherry trees. So begins a journey that I have been making at least once a week for several years on my way to the counselling agency where I offer sessions.

I love this walk at almost any time of year, not least because it keeps me in touch with the seasons, but my favourite time is the spring, when the buds on the cherry trees slowly swell and eventually break into the most fabulous blossom, creating a spectacular floral gallery along which to walk. As the short-lived blossom passes its peak and the petals fall, I always feel a twinge of sadness. And then I forget what has been lost and begin instead to take pleasure in the way this parkland is used in the summer. In fine weather, its acres of grass are dotted with people, some reading or sunbathing on their own, others in small groups apparently enjoying each other's company over barbecues, ball games and whatever else takes their fancy. As the summer passes and the academic year begins, I observe students moving to and fro between the university's central campus and the neighbourhoods in which they live. Autumn comes, the colours change, and with them the clocks. Now I am making this journey in fading light, witnessing the leaves fall and be whipped by the wind and scattered far and wide across the grass. As the year comes to an end, it is dark when I leave my office and often the depths of winter are still to come. Snow rarely settles here but, if it does, the transformation is extraordinary. The wildness of winter may bring down trees, or at least substantial boughs, but at its depths, light is also returning. As it does so, the crocuses break through and then the daffodils. Soon I will be noticing the buds swell once more on the cherry trees.

Whatever the time of year, on this walk I usually find myself shrugging off with relative ease whatever concerns my day in the office might have brought, somehow opening up a sense of space inside. I associate this sense of spaciousness with the movement of my body and my embodied knowledge of the pleasure of this journey. Many times, before I reach the cherry trees, I experience a frisson of anxiety and glance at my watch, mentally checking once again that I am on my way in plenty of time for my first session. I've noticed that this moment has become a habit, as if I somehow need to make contact with my fallibility and my capacity for anxiety. With that moment over, the walk usually becomes more meditative, and I may find one of my clients coming to my mind. I like just to let this happen. And then a more self-observing, reflecting part of my mind comes into play, noticing who comes to mind and who does not. I also sometimes have a sense – very hard to put into words – of someone I am working with taking up less space in me than I might expect. It is always that way around because those who seem to need a lot of space inside me have already made their presence felt. At the same time as these thoughts come and go, I remain in contact with my environment. I notice what is around me; I obey the ordinary norms entailed in sharing urban space with myriad strangers. But this is habitual behaviour, so well-practised that most of the time the intelligence it requires seems to be distributed throughout my body, rather than requiring of me any active thought. It does not conflict with my sense of inner spaciousness.

My journey continues beyond the limits of the park. I walk along city streets, passing shops and cafés until I reach my destination, some 35 minutes after leaving my office. During the second half of my walk, I tend to be more outwardly alert, because of moving vehicles and the constraints of a pavement, and correspondingly less inwardly meditative. This meditative quality also eludes me in seriously inclement weather, when my bodily movement requires effort and concentration that I otherwise take for granted. However, this journey in its entirety has long been an important transitional time and space for me. In transiting from university office to counselling agency, and from one urban neighbourhood to another, I also transit inside from academic to counsellor. That shift is not from one role to another – I don't experience being an academic or a counsellor as a role I put on or take off at will. It is more about a sense of which parts of me come to the fore.

I am an inveterate walker. Since I was a child, I have associated walking with its impacts on my mind. Sometimes walking slows down my racing thoughts or calms me when I feel troubled; sometimes walking releases something that feels stuck; sometimes walking is deeply meditative. In these ways, I find that, 'while walking, [my] body and mind can work together, so that thinking becomes almost a physical, rhythmic act' (Solnit, 2014: xv). Rebecca Solnit continues wryly: 'So much for the Cartesian mind/body divide,' hinting instead at an understanding of thinking that has affinities with Wilfred Bion's. For Bion (1962), thinking depends on the capacity to process somatic and sensory experience, a function that evolves during early life, initially undertaken by care-givers and, all going well, gradually internalised by the infant. In his account, calming a distressed baby through ordinary physical, emotional and mental activities sets in train the capacity to make experience available to thought. In my walking, I make comparable use of my motor skills to influence my internal state and achieve this expansion of capacity. Integral to this is my use of contact with the outdoor environment, especially that of the parkland, as if it stands in the place of my long internalised earliest care-givers in their nurturing of my infant self.

Walking always happens somewhere and, as I have described, the environment impacts on my body, my sensory experience and my thinking. This interface between an external environment and internal experience, especially in the context of urban walking, is claimed, at least by some, as the stuff of psychogeography. For example, Merlin Coverley (2010: 10) asserts that 'psychogeography is, as the name suggests, the point at which psychology and geography collide'. In how my walking contributes to my practice as a counsellor/psychotherapist (I use the terms interchangeably), am I a psychogeographer? In addressing this question, can I speak more broadly to the relationship between psychotherapy and psychogeography?

Coverley's appeal to a collision between psychology and geography is important to how psychogeography is understood: some sense of disruption, confrontation or dissonance reverberates through much writing in, of and about psychogeography, which generally seeks to disturb taken-for-granted ways of inhabiting and experiencing urban environments. Stories of the term typically point to Guy Debord's coinage in the context of the Situationist International, and locate the idea in an artistic and theoretical tradition that includes Charles Baudelaire's description of the *flâneur*, Walter Benjamin's Arcades Project, the Dadaist 'event', the Surrealist movement and Michel de Certeau's account of urban walking (for examples of these stories, see Bassett, 2004; Bonnett, 2017; Coverley, 2010; Plant, 1992; Richardson, 2015). The radical potential envisioned by Benjamin, Debord, de Certeau and others lay in the possibility of resisting, countering and subverting the dominant logics of capitalist cities, which, often invisibly, serve the interests of the powerful. For de Certeau (1984), the ordinary, everyday practice of walking contrasts with and eludes the planning and administration of urban space and instead 'uses and reworks spaces while remaining itself opaque' to the view from above implicit in all maps and plans (Pinder, 2011: 676).

The park I cross at the beginning of my journey is administered and maintained by the city and has long been divided by surfaced paths, along which the majority of those traversing the park walk. We are channelled, obeying rather than reworking the formal plan. Nothing prevents me from walking on the grass but to reach the pedestrian traffic lights towards which I am heading, the path is the most convenient route. So, while I may be actively engaging with urban space, I do so rather predictably; my use is not opaque – I conform. For Tina Richardson (2015: 18), I cannot be a psychogeographer if the purpose of my walking is to get from A to B, which it is. Nor, she argues, are many other very ordinary reasons why people might walk, such as going for a stroll or going shopping, included within the scope of psychogeography. Will Self (2007) refuses to privilege an apparent absence of destination, but nevertheless he uses walking with consciously non-conformist intent: for example, in his efforts to walk to and from airports as well as to observe the spaces he traverses in fresh and unexpected ways. As well as being rather different from my walk from university office to counselling agency, this also differs from de Certeau's (1984) account of walking as an intrinsically creative everyday practice in which conscious intentionality is irrelevant because we never know what might happen in our fortuitous encounters in urban space. From this point of view, by staying on the path today, I may conform, but other possibilities always remain available. Indeed, as I have described, my pleasure in this walk is heightened by the variability ensured by the changing weather and seasons, as well as the variability of my own musings.

Nevertheless, an emphasis on intentionally seeking a perspective that somehow goes 'against the grain' seems to be central to psychogeography (Bonnett, 2017). I worry about this demand for intentionality, especially when linked to the exclusion of ordinary forms of walking, because it unwittingly sets boundaries around psychogeography that can be used to police it, enrolling it into a disciplinary frame, which seems to me diametrically opposed to the provocations of many of its self-defined practitioners, from Guy Debord to Iain Sinclair. Unless its vagueness can be tolerated, I am excluded from its scope.

There are also other reasons why I may not belong on the terrain of psychogeography. In going against the grain, 'the walker connects with the terrain in a way that sets her- or himself up as a critic of the space under observation' (Richardson, 2015: 18). This conception of the walker as an anonymous, critical observer of urban life is implicitly masculine, originating in the possibilities opened up for men (with the luxury of time) to stroll and spectate in 19th century European cities, epitomised at least initially by Paris. As feminist writers have long argued, vision and the gaze are gendered: the possibility of being an observer of urban space privileges a masculine subject position (Mulvey, 1973; Rose, 1993). This does not preclude women from taking up the position of observer, but in its 19th century origins the *flâneur* was indubitably male and the object of his gaze – whether people or things, whether overtly sexualised or not – was implicitly feminised (Wolff, 1985; Wilson, 1991). Consequently, navigating urban space has often been perceived to be much more fraught for women than for men, and the female *flâneur*, or *flâneuse*, might be equated with or mistaken for the prostitute (Coverley, 2010), notwithstanding numerous examples of women who walk the city for a multitude of other reasons (Elkin, 2016), including psychogeographic ones (Rose, 2015).

Urban space is also 'raced', perhaps most violently in cities in the US. This goes some way to explain why so many of the widely-cited authors and proponents of psychogeography are white men, although it should also be noted that publishing and promotional activities have tended to eclipse or write out the contributions of women (Bridger, 2013; Elkin, 2016; Knowles, 2009), and the same is true of non-white men, transgender people, disabled people and others routinely 'othered' by dominant social norms. The sense in which a normative masculine subject position is embedded in psychogeography troubles and alienates me and pushes me towards other ways of working with and thinking about the interface between psychology and geography.

And yet, if we return to the idea of a collision between psychology and geography, perhaps what is understood by psychogeography might be widened and recast. Notwithstanding her emphasis on psychogeographers as observers of urban space, Richardson (2015: 18) also argues that they simultaneously 'unite with it through the sensorial acknowledgement of its omnipresence. The space becomes momentarily transformed through this relationship'. This statement draws attention to both embodied experience and a deeply relational understanding of space, each of which I reflect on in turn, suggesting the potential for closer links between some ideas implicit in psychogeography and psychotherapy. It is also worth noting that psychotherapy, like psychogeography, came into existence in a European urban context, with key features of urban life intrinsic to its framing (Bondi, 2009). For example, it requires that the only relationship between client and practitioner is their professional one, which assumes a high degree of segmentation in the ways in which people interact with each other, characteristic of much urban life, and this makes possible the boundaried qualities of the therapeutic relationships offered to those consulting counsellors and psychotherapists.

The sense of interior spaciousness I experience on my journey from university office to counselling agency speaks to my capacity to symbolise feelings or emotions sensed in and through my body. My chosen phrase – interior spaciousness – is informed by the particular cultural resources I bring to the task of giving words to feelings, including my long familiarity with the fields of human geography and psychoanalysis. I also appeal to senses among and beyond the traditional five. Vision appears in my appreciation of the scene I describe; I imagine the sound of the wind; through my sense of touch, I feel the impact of the weather via skin exposed to the elements or hidden below layers of clothing, and through its physical force on my moving body. The tactile is interwoven with sights, sounds, smells and even the taste of the air in different seasons. When I refer to the movement of my body in space, I appeal to proprioception, and my sensing of internal states might be understood as exemplifying interoception.

These sensory capacities, together with my active use of them, contribute to my experience of thinking as an embodied practice. They are central to my way of being a psychotherapist. In the consulting room, I draw extensively on embodied sensation as an integral aspect of what happens in my mind, and this itself feeds into my sense, when walking, of intelligence distributed throughout my body. Psychogeographers valorise the capacity to notice the environments with which they engage in fresh and creative ways. It seems to me that therapeutic training and practice might constitute ways of preparing people to do this, especially in relation to symbolising the bodily impress of sensory experience. In the opening paragraphs of this chapter, my attention lies with my body in outdoor urban space; in the consulting room, I draw on the same senses and sensibilities to attune myself to the relational dynamics of the therapeutic space.

Psychogeography is widely understood as a way of investigating and intervening in the environments in which people live and work. These environments are conceptualised as external to their human inhabitants and generally 'outside' rather than inside homes and workplaces. They are viewed as channelling, constraining, disciplining and limiting human behaviour in ways that endorse the status quo. Hence psychogeographers' aspirations to reveal 'hidden topographical layers of social history' (Richardson, 2015: 18) and to expose underlying power structures. But the boundary between person and place is permeable, acknowledged in Richardson's reference to a sense of becoming one with the space the psychogeographer explores, and to the potential, if momentary, transformation of that space. For much psychogeography, this requires acts or events that challenge the norms governing behaviour in urban space: for example, by following the path of a motorway on foot (Sinclair, 2002) or through an impromptu serenade of street music and dancing in New York (Pinder, 2005). The feel or ambience of the place changes through such interventions, and therefore the way it is experienced by its users changes too.

As a psychotherapist, I too engage intentionally with the physical environments in which I practice, but rather than seeking to expose and challenge social norms inscribed within an external environment, I am more interested in tracking what might be happening at that permeable boundary between person and place. To illuminate what I mean by this, I return to the moment at which I arrive at the counselling agency to which I have walked. I press the buzzer, announce myself via the intercom, and the door releases. I step inside and check in with the office staff. This process is familiar to me, and it is much the same for the clients who come to this place. Announcing myself via the intercom is anxiety-provoking for me and I imagine often more so for many clients. Will my voice be heard above the traffic noise behind me? Will my name be recognised and admission granted by the invisible door-keeper within? Can I tolerate the swirling emotions accompanying these thoughts, including the sense of shame induced by the possibility of remaining unheard, unrecognised and excluded; the fleeting sense that I am not wanted here and must plead for admission; the accompanying rage that I am in this moment an abandoned outsider? I bear with these feelings, as do the clients I see; we get used to the ritual at the door, although sometimes in sessions I hear about the dread and anxiety it evokes. Noticing my own fleeting anxieties, which I could so easily brush aside, helps me maintain the possibility of what Paula Heimann (1950: 82) described as 'a freely roused emotional sensibility', and therefore my capacity to follow empathically the feelings a client may be communicating.

One day in my own therapy, I rang the bell at the door to my therapist's consulting room in the usual way, but no one came. Eventually, I rang the bell again and this time my ring was heard. The door opened and I promptly forgot all about my anxious wait outside; I remembered it suddenly only at the end of the next session. I swiftly recognised a connection to an experience I had at the age of six when I had felt inconsolably abandoned. But, just as important for me is how I initially forgot what had happened to me and in me during my wait outside the door to my therapist's consulting room. Without any awareness that I was doing so, I had banished the feelings stirred in me from my awareness, perhaps unconsciously deeming them 'too much' or somehow unacceptable. While a couple of sessions later I was able to recall my feelings, it is experiences like these of how I banish things from my mind that make the concept of unconscious life central to my approach to practice.

The feelings I associate with coming to the door and requesting admission are stimulated by my interaction with my external environment and speak volumes about my inner world. Like that moment when I glance at my watch early in my walk, my capacity for anxiety comes to the fore. But something else happens too. No longer am I moving through urban space enveloped in my sense of being an independent, autonomous human being; now I am thrown into a dependent relationship with an invisible, momentarily impersonal other. The dread-full questions that arise in me in response to my utter, if momentary, dependence on another break into my meditative state and the internal spaciousness I have described contracts. Until this moment, I was enjoying the expansive protection of what Winnicott (1971: 2) calls an intermediate area 'to which inner reality and external life both contribute... an area not to be challenged, because no claim is made on its behalf except that it shall exist as a resting-place for the individual engaged in the perpetual human task of keeping inner and outer reality separate yet interrelated'. Now, all of a sudden, my resting place feels perilously flimsy and I am in contact with my ontological insecurity (Bondi, 2014; Laing, 1965). The moment passes as I pass the threshold, but this time I do not forget it.

To the psychogeographer, my reflections on entering the building might be read as opening up a challenge to the agency's arrangements for 'greeting' those who seek to enter, and perhaps as a springboard for criticising the privatisation and securitisation of urban space (Blomley, 2004; Lippert & Walby, 2013; Mitchell, 2003). But that is not my purpose here. I know very well that this entry system has been considered carefully and is not imposed thoughtlessly. Another arrangement would also induce feelings in those arriving at this building and I want to work with whatever is thrown up in me and those with whom I work.

Psychogeographers do not often pay much attention to interior environments. For me, while walking outside is of considerable personal importance, it is often interior spaces that call my attention in my therapeutic practice. The building I enter is on one level, the low-ceilinged interior opening out from a narrow and inconspicuous street frontage. I think it is a bit womb-like. It is quiet but not silent, peaceful but not placid. As soon as it is free, I go to the room in which I see clients. It is light and airy, simply furnished from somewhere like IKEA, closer to homely than business-like, but also impersonal, nondescript, functional and not much different from the other consulting rooms in this building. However, alongside the standard-issue chairs and neutral décor, there are details that speak of careful attention, like the vase in each room with some garden flowers or attractive foliage or pussy willow, something living and fragile, which are refreshed every few days. So, alongside the impersonal feel, this is a space that is thought about and cared about long before I arrive and long after I leave. That small vase with greenery of some kind connects this indoor space to the outside world and the built environment to the natural world. In so doing, it seems to me to facilitate the traffic between interior and exterior landscapes that reverberates through therapeutic work (Bondi with Fewell, 2003).

I plump the cushions and check to see that everything is as it should be, perhaps turn on a lamp or open a window. In moments, the room becomes a space that is mine, not exclusively but sufficiently for me to feel at home in it, to inhabit it, to feel that I will be held by it. For the next few hours, this room will act as container for me as well as the clients I work with. I take it for granted, depending absolutely on its stability, its predictability and its familiarity, which support my capacity not just to listen but to be as fully present as I can, to receive and to register whatever might come my way. The receptivity and creative sense of presence that I cultivate inside me are possibilities that I can draw upon in many different spaces and places, but I cannot do so without feeling trusting and confident of my environment. My capacity for welcoming moments of contact with my vulnerabilities and insecurities depends on my sense of also being securely held, and this holding is simultaneously and integrally both internal and external.

Again, it is Winnicott's writings to which I turn to conceptualise the way I experience and make use of the space in which I practise. In much of Winnicott's writing, the analyst with his or her analysand is frequently equated with the mother and her infant, a view perhaps implicit in my description of the interior space of the agency as womb-like. More specifically, I draw on the room and its furnishings as a 'facilitating environment' (Winnicott, 1965). In claiming the space as 'mine', I hint at a sense of feeling that it exists within an area of my 'omnipotent control', where I can take it for granted and know it will survive the use I make of it. I appeal here to Winnicott's (1971) concept of 'using an object' that I consume and destroy in my active, ruthless presumption upon it, remaining confident in its capacity to survive. For Winnicott, the capacity to use an object is achieved developmentally in the relationship between infant and carer; his concept of 'the facilitating environment' seems to me to be something of an invitation to psychogeographers and others to extend the application of his theories beyond the interpersonal, human world into a more-than-human world that encompasses the multitudinous elements of our environments (see Latham (1999) for one such application and Abram (1996) on the 'more-than-human').

Having 'taken possession' of my consulting room, I am ready to meet my first client. I walk to the waiting area and, on seeing me, my client stands up. Now we walk together along the corridor to my/our room. This meeting and short journey is accompanied by greetings in the form of eye contact and proceeds in silence or with a few spoken words. With someone I have worked with for a while, this micro-journey has a familiar feel to it, and I will be alert to anything that cuts into that familiarity. With someone new, it is different, and I will hold somewhere in me how they register on my senses the very first time I meet them, and return to it later on. I wonder if I might think of this as therapeutically-informed, 'indoor' psychogeography in action.

In the room I shut the door, making sure that it has closed completely. A basic requirement for therapeutic work is a private space, as free from intrusions as possible, in which the client's confidentiality is carefully held. In here there are no prying eyes; if a phone rings or pings, it will be the client's and not mine. Preventing sounds from intruding is harder, and if voices coming from outside can be heard inside, my client and I may wonder if our voices can be heard by others beyond these four walls. So, the boundaries around the space are not perfect and we work with the flaws rather than ignoring them, again attending to the impact of this environment on our feelings and thoughts.

Just as I deployed my senses on my journey here, so I use my senses again now I am with my client. Like psychogeographers, I observe, noticing details such as how my client comes into and occupies this space and, crucially, what feelings are evoked in me. My attention is simultaneously internal and external, always apprehended through my psyche-soma, a concept Winnicott (1958) used in his writing to convey his understanding of the inextricability of what has, at least since Descartes, too often and unhelpfully been understood as a distinction between mind and body. So it is more accurate to say that I sense rather than consciously notice how one client seems to look around the room each time he arrives, commenting on any small change he spots and settling only once the ritual is complete, and how another might one day comment that the room seems bigger than usual today and I might wonder if she perhaps feels smaller. In these and myriad other ways, I aim to work in that intermediate area Winnicott (1971) describes, attending to the intersubjective and intrapsychic flow that unfolds within and around me.

In the room, we take our seats and there I leave what happens between me and my client. The pleasure I take in walking to the counselling agency is influenced by the prospect of being with the clients I am due to see in my capacity as their counsellor. Therapeutic work is work – sometimes exhausting and challenging but, for me and others like me, also deeply satisfying. At least one aspect of the satisfaction I feel comes from my sense of always integrating mind and body in my work. Winnicott's concept of psyche-soma was preceded by Freud's (1923) understanding of the ego as a body-ego. I understand the unconscious as necessarily bodily. In sessions, therefore, my listening, thinking and observing are first and foremost about feeling. I feel my way in each and every session, just as I feel my way through the urban environment I traverse to reach my destination, to cross the threshold of the space in which I work, and to make that space sufficiently my own to be ready to meet my client and offer them my capacity for therapeutic relating.

I've seen my final client for today. I make sure that I leave the room in order for the next counsellor who will be using it, my temporarily ruthless use of it now giving way to my sense of being part of a collective venture. I gather myself and my belongings to leave. Back out on the street, for half the year it is dark and for the other half it is still light. I retrace my steps for about 10 minutes and then turn off, making my way to the station. My state is often quite meditative again, although differently so than on my earlier journey. Often, I am tired. I may find myself thinking about something I have discovered or understood afresh during the last few hours, perhaps going back to a moment I had not consciously thought about at the time but for which sensations and images now come. While sometimes I find myself mulling over the final session of the day, it isn't unusual for something from an earlier session to demand my attention almost immediately, as if I had not been able to process it or pay it enough attention at the time. Sometimes I'll be acknowledging to myself something that I found tough, whether because of the content or the process. I am glad to have this time on my own among others, an anonymous urbanite on her way home. My overall sense of this walk is much vaguer than the earlier one, perhaps because so often it is already dark or nearly dark and I am done for the day, but also perhaps because I have so much inside me to process, generating a different kind of relationship between what I experience as inside and outside. That processing will continue throughout and beyond my journey home, perhaps into my dreams, carried in my body from the room in which I meet my clients into a multitude of other spaces.

The writings of psychogeography have given me something to play with. I am drawn to the field because it takes walking seriously and because that idea of a collision between psychology and geography makes some intuitive sense. But I baulk at some of its apparent assumptions, including its failure to trouble the white masculine privilege that has been inscribed within its theory and practice and its privileging of conscious intentionality over psychotherapeutically informed attention to routine. However, I feel more aligned with its interest in embodied and relational appreciations of space, which seem to me to have much to gain from psychotherapy, as I hope that my musings illustrate. In my account, I have stayed upright, on my two feet, leaving my therapeutic work at the moment my client and I sit down. What a paradox that I wrote these words sitting at a desk. But I frequently broke off from that position, finding that I often needed to feel the weight of my body on my two feet and to return to the rhythmic movement of placing one foot in front of another. Perhaps something of that motion makes its presence felt in this text.

## References

Abram D (1996). *The Spell of the Sensuous: perception and language in the more than human world.* New York, NY: Pantheon.

Bassett K (2004). Walking as an aesthetic practice and critical tool: some psychogeographic experiments. *Journal of Geography in Higher Education* 28(3): 397–410.

Bion W (1962). The psycho-analytic study of thinking. *International Journal of Psycho-Analysis 43*: 306–310.

Blomley N (2004). *Unsettling the City: urban land and the politics of property*. New York, NY: Routledge.

Bondi L (2014). Feeling insecure: a personal account in a psychoanalytic voice. *Social and Cultural Geography 15*(3): 332–350.

Bondi L (2009). Counselling in rural Scotland: care, proximity and trust. *Gender, Place and Culture 16*(2): 163–179.

Bondi L, with Fewell J (2003). 'Unlocking the cage door': the spatiality of counselling. *Social and Cultural Geography 4*(4): 527–547.

Bonnett A (2017). The enchanted path: magic and modernism in psychogeographical walking. *Transactions of the Institute of British Geography 42*(3): 472–484.

Bridger AJ (2013). Psychogeography and feminist methodology. *Feminism and Psychology 23*(3): 285–298.

Coverley M (2010). *Psychogeography*. Harpenden: Pocket Essentials.

De Certeau M (1984). *The Practice of Everyday Life*. Berkeley, CA: University of California Press.

Elkin L (2016). *Flâneuse: women walk the city in Paris, New York, Tokyo, Venice and London*. London: Chatto and Windus.

Freud S (1923/1961). The ego and the id and other works. *The Standard Edition of the Complete Psychological Works of Sigmund Freud, Vol 19* (J Strachey, ed). London: Hogarth Press (pp1–66).

Heimann P (1950). On counter-transference. *International Journal of Psycho-Analysis 31*: 81–84.

Knowles D (2009). Claiming the streets: feminist implications of psychogeography as a business research method. *The Electronic Journal of Business Research Methods 7*(1): 47–54.

Laing RD (1965). *The Divided Self*. Harmondsworth: Penguin.

Latham A (1999). Powers of engagement: on being engaged, being indifferent and urban life. *Area 31*(2): 161–168.

Lippert RK, Walby K (eds) (2013). *Policing Cities: urban securitization and regulation in a twenty-first century world*. Abingdon: Routledge.

Mitchell D (2003). *The Right to the City*. New York, NY: Guilford Press.

Mulvey L (1973). Visual pleasure and narrative cinema. *Screen 16*(3): 2–18.

Pinder D (2011). Errant paths: the poetics and politics of walking. *Environment and Planning D: Society and Space 29*(4): 672–692.

Pinder D (2005). Arts of urban exploration. *Cultural Geographies 12*(4): 383–411.

Plant S (1992). *The Most Radical Gesture: the Situationist International in a postmodern age*. Abington: Routledge.

Richardson T (2015). Introduction. In: Richardson T (ed). *Contemporary British Psychogeography*. London: Rowman and Littlefield (pp1–28).

Rose G (1993). *Feminism and Geography: the limits of geographical knowledge*. Cambridge: Polity Press.

Rose M (2015). Confessions of an anarcho-flâneuse of psychogeography the Mancunian way. In: Richardson T (ed). *Contemporary British Psychogeography*. London: Rowman and Littlefield (pp147–162).

Self W (2007). *Psychogeography*. New York, NY: Bloomsbury.

Sinclair I (2002). *London Orbital*. London: Granta.

Solnit R (2014). *Wanderlust: a History of Walking*. London: Granta.

Wilson E (1991). *The Sphinx and the City*. London: Virago.

Winnicott DW (1971). *Playing and Reality*. London: Routledge.

Winnicott DW (1965). *The Maturational Processes and the Facilitating Environment*. London: Hogarth Press.

Winnicott DW (1958). *Through Paediatrics to Psycho-Analysis: collected papers*. London: Tavistock Publications.

Wolff J (1985). The invisible flâneuse: women and the literature of modernity. *Theory, Culture and Society* 2(3): 37–46.

Paradise Cmrs                                    19·08·17

# 6 | Loitering, resisting and moving
## Morag Rose

We can't agree on what psychogeography means, but we all like plants growing out of the side of the buildings, looking at things from new angles, radical history, drinking tea and getting lost; having fun and feeling like a tourist in your home town. Gentrification, advertising and blandness make us sad. We believe there is magick in the Mancunian rain. Our city is wonderful and made for more than shopping. We want to reclaim it for play and revolutionary fun. On the first Sunday of the month we go for a wander of some sort and we also organise occasional festivals, exhibitions, shows, spectacles, silliness and other random shenanigans. Please come and join us, everyone is welcome.

So reads the text on a flyer from the Loiterers Resistance Movement (LRM), a Manchester-based psychogeographical collective set up in 2006 by, among others, Morag Rose. In this chapter, she discusses with Chris Rose (no, we're not related) the ethos, ideas and activities of the LRM.

**CR:** The word 'loitering' is linked in my mind with the phrase 'with intent'. It's a word with some negative connotations, but maybe that's why you chose it?

**MR:** Yes, we wanted to question the notion that loitering is inherently negative. Asserting the value of the public space has always been central to our aim, and we wanted to slow down, critically engage with and celebrate the idea of being in and exploring space.

The LRM was born from an Anarchist social centre in Manchester called The Basement. This was a collectively run community space that aimed to be a non-commercial haven in the neoliberal city. The Basement housed a radical bookshop and library, an opensource computer hub, a meeting space, gallery and a vegan café, and was created as somewhere to hatch plans, discuss radical politics and make new connections. The LRM wanted to extend that onto the streets in a playful way, using psychogeography as a way to start conversations and engage a wider group of people in art, activism and political debate. The idea of creative mischief always appealed to me, alongside the idea of transforming the everyday into something enchanting.

We actually struggled for a while to find a name, and only really adopted one when we organised an exhibition of DIY maps and art called 'The First Accidental International Festival of Psychogeography'. I wasn't keen on having 'psychogeography' in the group's title as it can be alienating, and also has negative connotations of its own. We wanted a three-word name as it was a hat tip to inspirations such as MAP (Manchester Area Psychogeographic), the LPA (London Psychogeographical Association) and the AAA (Association of Autonomous Astronauts). It also made clear this was a collective rather than an individual exploration; our events are always co-created by everyone who walks with us. One day a friend, who was about to leave Manchester, said she was going because 'if you loiter in Brisbane you get a sun tan, if you loiter in Manchester you get an ASBO', and that was that, we found our name. The other two words fitted with our socio-political context and I like the idea of not just resisting criminalisation of loitering but also slowing down, challenging the urge for speed and industry as a resistant act in and of itself. The closest we ever came to a membership card was an ink stamp someone made us that said, 'Loitering With Intent to Make Manchester Wonderful'. We also called our 10th anniversary exhibition 'Loitering With Intent: The Art and Politics of Walking', so we have played with that phrase a bit too.

The group has evolved over the years but at heart our aims are still the same.

## Psychogeographical origins

**CR**: You say '... psychogeography has negative connotations of its own'. Say more!

**MR**: My initial reservations were about accessible language. We really wanted the LRM to be open to everyone. We wanted to be true to the idea of a revolution of everyday life and blur boundaries between theory, practice, artist, activist, academic etc. An invitation full of jargon didn't seem like a helpful starting point for that. I should probably add, we were a lot more ramshackle and ad hoc than this may make us sound. The LRM was just one of many projects and was/is as much about us learning and exploring as well. Action came before a lot of the theory for me, and some of the other problems with psychogeography only became apparent to me later. If I had known about the *flâneur*, or issues around race, gender, disability etc, I would have been even more hesitant.

In retrospect we were quite idealistic, but I never anticipated that the LRM would still be walking together and become such a profound experience for me. We embodied a DIY ethos: don't wait for permission, create something and see what happens. I believed then, as I do now, that psychogeography is much more diverse and interesting than stereotypes would suggest. You got in touch after reading my chapter in *Walking Inside Out: contemporary British psychogeography* (Richardson, 2015), in which Tina Richardson brought together a range of perspectives that demonstrate this richness. I've always wanted inclusion and access to be at the heart of what the LRM does. This manifests itself in lots of ways, and is one of the reasons our events are always free and open to anyone to attend. If a central tenet is that the streets should belong to everyone, we need to put that into practice with every step possible.

**CR**: Yes, *Walking Inside Out* had a big impact on me. It helped me get past some of my own assumptions about psychogeography, but the stereotypes still need challenging, I think. So, tell us about the *flâneur*. Is that a sort of loiterer? And what are the other problems that you see with psychogeography?

**MR**: The *flâneur* is an archetype, a lone male wanderer of immense privilege: wealthy, cis, able-bodied, educated, white, a hegemonic 'ideal' type. He passes through space, observing and absorbing but never touching or being touched by anyone or anything. Although he has some merit in literature – for example, in the work of Walter Benjamin (1999) – he has been taken too literally and often haunts conversations about psychogeography and walking art, reflecting patriarchal norms. His perceived dominance is largely to do with the established canon, as the actual reality of walking art is much more miscellaneous and remarkable.

Part of the issue is that many of those other voices operate under the mainstream media radar, producing and distributing work independently, and are often overshadowed by the celebrity usual suspects (of course, psychogeography is not alone in this). I think this recognition doesn't always reflect the quality of work, but rather the systems we operate in. For excellent examples of resistance to this, and reimagining the praxis, I would suggest looking at the Walking Women events[1] or listening to the radio programmes Jo Norcup's Geography Workshop have produced.[2] I could fill your book with a list of people and groups whose work inspires me. Not all of them would identify as psychogeographers (and some may actively dislike the term) but they are all using creative walking methods. They include Monique Besten, Jane Samuels, Nazli Tumedem, Phil Smith, Lucy Furlong, Laura Oldfield Ford, Clare Qualmann, Walkwalkwalk, Blake Morris, Dee Heddon, Writes and Sites, Jess Allen, Ceri Morgan, Victor Buehring, Sonia Overall, Kubra Khademi, Idit Nathan and Helen Stratford, Inua Ellams, Alison Lloyd – I could go on and on, and I know I will have forgotten some amazing names.

The male dominance personified in the *flâneur* is one aspect of the problem with the original incarnation of psychogeography. It often has an unpleasant colonial and exclusionary edge too. This can be detected in essentialist discourses of place when people talk

1. See www.walkingartistsnetwork.org/walking-women (accessed 24 April 2019).

2. See http://geographyworkshop.com/category/sounds/ (accessed 20 November 2018).

of owning, penetrating, conquering space; of othering different cultures, heroically exploring or 'discovering' communities; of imposing their own narrative onto somewhere, dominating and denying plurality. This must be acknowledged and challenged whenever we encounter it. But I do believe, despite these terrible issues, there is an idea, a concept, worth evolving. There is a problem too of obscure language, curiously at odds with a desire to engage with a wide audience, and this is another reason why the LRM did not have 'psychogeography' in our name, as we did not want to exclude through jargon.

**CR**: So, what do you think is the concept, or the ideas in psychogeography that are worth evolving in all of this?

**MR**: Obviously I think psychogeography itself is still worth exploring, although I do understand why some people are keen to invent new terms for it, and in some ways its contemporary evolutions are often very far removed from its roots. For me, the core idea is that walking can be transformational, that it can become a political and artistic tool, and that, through creative walking, we can understand, connect with and experience space in new ways. To be psychogeographical, there has to be a critical, political intention too. The *dérive* is not just a pleasant wander, although it may be fun and actually it was the ludic side that first attracted me.

**CR**: Can you tell me more about the back story of psychogeography and how you see its relevance today?

**MR**: The term was coined in 1955 by Guy Debord, who later became the de facto leader of the Situationist International (SI). They were an international neo-Marxist organisation with a fluid membership of artists, writers and intellectuals, active between 1957 and 1972 but most closely associated with the May 1968 insurrections in France. Psychogeography was only a very small part of their oeuvre; their wider aim was a total revolution and restructuring of society. Debord's major contribution was *The Society of the Spectacle* (1967/1992). In this he discusses how media and mediated representations distort and replace our authentic desires. The drives of capitalism mean we are constantly exploited, sold to and perpetually alienated. Debord was writing in a pre-internet age, but in a time when we are constantly bombarded by images, advertisements, propaganda, the question seems even more urgent. How can we experience unmediated pleasure and our true, authentic selves? Of course, whether this is ever truly possible is also debatable, and the notion of authenticity is another huge question, and I'm just skimming the surface here.

We are all tangled up in the system, and there is a constant struggle to avoid recuperation – the process by which capitalism takes rebellion, neuters it and sells it back to us. Think about, for example, how alternative music becomes diluted by the mainstream, or how feminist slogans are appropriated in advertising. The need to interrogate the media, to always ask who is trying to sell what to us and why, remains urgent, particularly since technology and capitalism have evolved since the SI were active. Society's obsession with mediated images has only deepened with the ubiquity of social media and a proliferation of screens.

The other key Situationist idea that I still think important is the need to dissolve boundaries between politics, activism, art etc. To cede power to politicians or corporations is dangerous; it damages us all, and we need to cultivate mutual aid, solidarity and co-operation. If we are ruled by millionaires, well, how can we expect them to understand, for example, the impact of cuts to the NHS, the experience of poverty or the lived experiences of austerity? We deserve better, and we need to take back control. Frustratingly, much of Vaneigem's *The Revolution of Everyday Life* (1967) remains pertinent and inspiring today.

## Loitering

**CR:** Who are the present-day loiterers? Do you think they have different motivations?

**MR:** If you are talking about the folk who come along to LRM events, they are a fairly mixed bunch. We don't all share the same artistic or political tastes but there is a common sense of curiosity, a love for the hidden stories of Manchester, and a sense of wonder in the mundane environment. We mostly veer towards the left, unsurprisingly given our origins, and we share a critical engagement with the dominant narratives of regeneration. I am sure some are motivated mostly by the joy of conversation and connection that walking together brings, and others want to join us to bear witness to and record the changing environment.

Our walks are convivial; they are co-produced and directed by whoever turns up on the day, and people wander in and out over the months, depending on their other commitments. I'm happy that no one seems to come just once, and it's a great pleasure when a loiterer drifts back after months away. Thinking about the people who came on our last event, they included students, artists, people who work in offices, warehouses, classrooms, advice centres and shops, as well as unemployed and retired people. Of course, none are defined by their jobs but it's one way of describing their diverse perspectives.

I think we all share a love of the urban and a desire for a fairer, more equitable society. Walking together will not save the world (I assume) but loitering is only one small part of everyone's lives, and everyone has many interesting stories to tell about the other things they do. I see us as a small part of a much larger network of people interested in the same things, who believe that the streets should belong to everyone and that creative walking has transformative potential.

**CR**: Is loitering a safe activity? It sounds potentially dangerous, especially for women.

**MR**: LRM walks are communal. The group offers a kind of safety and an implicit permission to experiment and play. Our collective ethos means we take care of ourselves and each other, stop when someone is uncomfortable, keep pace with the slowest etc. I am aware the group offers affordances to walk where you might not dare go alone – for example, along isolated canal towpaths. During research for my thesis, many women told me how much they loved the atmosphere along the canals but felt constrained in venturing down there alone. I hope walking together can banish some demons through familiarity.

However, this is a difficult question in so many ways. I know sometimes I may sound naive when I speak about how we should take to the streets and claim our space in the city. I know in reality this is more difficult for some people and I don't want to gloss over these inequalities. As a woman, I have personally been hassled and harassed many times and I know many others have worse experiences because of intersectional factors amplifying abuse such as racism, Islamophobia and transphobia. We must challenge this at every opportunity.

I do believe one of the biggest threats we face is being too scared to go out, and I want to interrogate and challenge the construction of fear. Most people, most of the time, in most of Manchester are good people and do not intend to cause harm. That does not mean fearfulness or caution is unjustified. I know I have absorbed warnings from many sources – friends, family, the media, popular culture etc. I also know my physical limitations when faced with a threat, when all the statistical evidence or feminist rhetoric will not save me. However still I walk, because the alternative is unthinkable. I refuse to stay in, but also my personal experiences of the city tell me it is mostly OK outside. Still, though, I take precautions; women everywhere will know the stance I am talking about when I say that, when walking alone at night, I keep my head up, alert, my pace quickens, my keys are in my hand, I stay in the light when I can. There are of course other dangers too – traffic, pollution, trip hazards etc – but these are part of urban life that we live with despite the inconvenience.

## Resistance

**CR**: Can I ask you about 'resisting' now? What are you resisting? Is there a unified goal or are different people resisting different things?

**MR**: I think we all broadly share the same concerns, although we have different perspectives on them, and our personal priorities may be a bit different. Broadly, the problems are around the neoliberal city: growing inequality, alienation, privatisation, marketisation and commodification. A long list of interrelated words but, as our manifesto says, 'We believe the streets are for more than shopping.' Loitering, playing, not spending money – these should not be radical acts, but they can become so if we lose the concept of public space and focus only on profit. I think we are also resisting boredom, heterogeneity and the construction of fear.

This underlying commitment to the common good, and to imagining a future, is one way the *dérive* is different to other kinds of walking. It should be an open, affective walk, and perhaps one of the more important things it resists is an essentialism. We view space as plural, open and, as Doreen Massey suggests (2005), a constellation of stories-so-far. Massey wasn't a psychogeographer, but her work is important to me and the LRM. She perceived places as networks of relationships that stretch across local, national and global borders. There is always a power dimension to this; Massey was very attentive to inequalities and the possibility of change. Her relational model means places are always contingent, evolving and in flux. It's an elegant and progressive conception of place that suggests we can love where we live but still reach out. We can also change the future shape of places, and society itself, by paying attention to those power relationships and the narratives we create around them.

It occurs to me, talking to you, that isolating the words like this makes our name somewhat absurd, and that is not a bad thing. Resistance feels such a strong word. Really, we are starting a conversation with each other, and with space, resisting disconnection I suppose.

**CR**: It is strange, in a way, looking at the LRM one word at a time. But I'm thinking of it as a sort of group – three characters, L, R and M, who all have their own characteristics. Then, when you put them together in a group, they bounce off one another, resonate and reveal aspects that were impossible to see in isolation.

**MR**: I really like the way you have framed that – letters, ideas bouncing off of each other. To be truthful, I'm not sure as much thought was put into our name. I wanted three words, as it seemed to fit with a convention I liked, and it needed something to convey the collective nature of the work we wanted to do.

**CR**: I feel I've got to know the L character a bit, and now I'm finding out about R. Can you tell me some specific examples of the ways in which resistance is carried out? Is it ever risky?

**MR**: We work at a very micro, local level (although links with others mean these may happen in other locations too). As I said, something like walking across the grass, talking to a stranger or smelling plastic flowers does not, should not, feel like resistance. I suppose some of the most obvious acts of defiance are playing CCTV Bingo or organising performative walks that highlight the erosion of public space. CCTV Bingo is a pertinent example of our approach, because I wanted to create a non-didactic way of discussing securitisation. I have a deep concern about the proliferation of security services and the psychological impact of constant surveillance.

I was provoked to action by a horrible, fearmongering poster from the British Transport Police that suggested looking at cameras was nefarious or somehow criminal. I think to be engaged in your environment, alert, asking questions, is a positive thing and I wanted to resist demonisation. There is also evidence that CCTV merely displaces, rather than solves crime. I also appreciate some people have genuine fears and sometimes, in some places, a camera makes you feel safe. So, I designed a game where you hunt for different kinds of cameras and your walk is guided by their gaze. Playing is perfectly legal and safe as long as you are sensible – for example, don't stand in the middle of the road, keep to public streets etc. As with all our events, we have a collective ethos about taking care of ourselves and each other. This is explicit in the gamecard instructions and implicit in all we do – for example, we walk in a group, at a pace that suits all, and everyone has a voice that is respected when deciding where to go.

Is it risky? Not really. Perhaps I look ridiculous sometimes, but that's not really a problem. Deconstructing fear was one of my central aims, and there is a confidence from walking together that encourages exploration and offers support. The risks we face are the same that anyone faces: traffic, trip hazards, bad weather etc. From very early on, I wanted to try to bridge a gap between different groups who all share broadly similar aims to make Manchester a kinder, more equitable and interesting place. The street, and public space, is an arena for encountering differences and, as I am sure many people have told you, walking and talking together can help break down hierarchies and start conversations in and with space. I didn't want to engage in actions that would stop some people feeling able to join in our conversations because they felt it was too high a risk for them, and I was very aware that many traditional forms of activism are exclusionary. For example, if you are precariously employed, have caring responsibilities or health concerns or are at risk of deportation, then you have solid reasons to be wary of attending an illegal action. Of course, you are still an active citizen with views and desires and we wanted to open up the public, political conversation. To be clear, I am not arguing against direct action or other forms of protest, just clarifying the origin of our 'First Sundays' meet-ups. I am also aware there is another important conversation about what it means to be radical now, but that is for another day.

**CR**: What do you see as the impact of your resistance?

**MR**: Hmm, this is really hard, and I don't know if I am the right person to answer. Leading on from your previous question, it is only one tool among many needed, and it would be disingenuous to make it sound more than it is. Everyone who walks with the LRM is much more than a loiterer, and they all do many things outside the *dérive* space. I do think walking together has an impact on a personal level, in the same way that art and conversations and friendships have an impact. Hamish Fulton says (Fulton, undated): 'A walk can exist like an invisible object in a complex world,' and I like that idea very much. I do think resonances linger and we add new stories to the city. We can also offer a different perspective on the everyday – an enchantment and an opening up. I also think there is value in persistence, in asking awkward questions and creating DIY maps. It may not be a huge shift in power but that does not make it insignificant. We can also be a catalyst for new links between people and place and I have always shared our resources as widely as possible to try and open up space for others.

**CR**: I agree that small gestures can, over time, alter attitudes and behaviours. A lot of my work has been in long-term psychotherapy and changing lives can seem as slow as changing the course of a river, but it happens.

## Movement

**CR**: It seems we have already got L and R in the room, so how about Movement? It's a word that has a big catchment area. I think of 'political' movements – Luddites, suffragettes, 'artistic' movements, Impressionism, Fauvism. Does this relate to the LRM?

**MR**: I hope it's clear from our conversations that we did have a political intention, certainly, and that remains our focus, but it has always been somewhat vague, mutable and (we hope) welcoming. Something else too – I wanted to be clear it wasn't 'my' group. We came from an Anarchist background, valuing non-hierarchical structures. Just as the group in a *dérive* changes direction and leader as it walks, so too has the LRM. For a while we shared all my internet passwords so anyone could post on the LRM website. Nothing bad happened, but I am more guarded with my personal data now. It would be disingenuous to claim total lack of hierarchy these days, when I do most of the admin and suchlike, but I am always open to ideas and offers to collaborate or for others to initiate a First Sunday.

So yes: Movement, but it could also have Association, Collective, Front or similar. I didn't expect still to be developing these ideas so many years later, and maybe if I did, the name would have been totally different. I wish I could tell you 'Movement' was chosen consciously because of its multiple meanings, because moving through space is how we live our theory, but that would be to retrofit a motive. The LRM was an experiment that is still being conducted. However, words do matter, and I am glad I have stood by (walked by?) this name.

**CR**: Movement, as you say, has multiple meanings, and now I'm thinking about walking – which is central to this book. Walking is not for everyone, though, is it?

**MR**: No, I suppose not, and it's interesting to think about why not. I've always strived to make clear that my definition of walking includes technologies such as wheelchairs, walking sticks and other mobility aids, and loitering itself is a very slow, deliberate, attentive type of walking. On a personal level, this reflects an inherent tension at the heart of my work as a walking artist/activist/academic/whatever it is I do. I have a progressive neurological condition, which means sometimes for me walking hurts. As a child, I spent time immobile in hospital and wore callipers. Today I am indebted to the NHS, including the too-often-overlooked magicians in orthotics and physiotherapy, for enabling me to keep going. At some point in my career, I will reflect more on this tension in a creative way but for now I would rather focus on wider issues. The social model of disability has some very important lessons that I think should be embedded in wider conversations, as it makes clear the problem is often a disabling environment rather than individual impairment.

There are, of course, many other reasons why, besides physical ability, people assume walking is not for them, and I think examining the reasons for this is important. Too often the built environment considers cars a priority, so pedestrians feel unsafe. This is reflected not just in the struggle to cross roads or the impact of air pollution but in the neglect of mundane infrastructures such as pavements. If the surface is full of potholes, blocked by cars or A-boards, poorly lit or covered in litter, these are just some reasons why walking is not appealing. These material factors are incredibly important in facilitating access and I think this should be viewed as a social justice issue. If you believe, as I do, that the streets belong to everyone and public space is common treasury, it follows they should be accessible to everyone.

We also need a more holistic view of access that includes issues such as street harassment. Every woman will have a cognitive map of places that feel unsafe to her, because she has experienced direct harassment or received warnings from friends, family or the wider culture that she will not be safe there. I use women as an example because my PhD research directly addresses this, but this abuse and restriction of access is intersectional, of course. The alarming resurgence of 'stop and search', with its racist overtones, is another example of a barrier to movement. Feeling able to walk freely in a landscape is dependent on many factors, and we are back again to the curse of the *flâneur* we discussed earlier.

**CR**: The 'curse of the *flâneur*' is a good name for this uncomfortable draught that blows through the book at various points! Moving on, however, another take on movement involves the passage through time – does this have any relevance here?

**MR**: Absolutely. Attentive walking is about attuning oneself to the hidden power structures of the city and these include historical forces and patterns. One of the dangers we face is a descent into nostalgia or becoming a local heritage group, because people (including me) do enjoy sharing stories and pointing out historical features. The Counter Tourism of Phil Smith (2010) is a much-needed reminder of how absurd and restrictive much heritage is. It is important to remember a *dérive* is not a predetermined route; it is about sensation and critical engagement. The LRM does do occasional tours, but we make it clear that our history is participatory, partial and personal. Examples of this include Manchester's Modernist Heroines, Drinking in the City (looking at cultural geographies of alcohol) and a guide to Liminal Spaces. These walks are always overtly performative and we try to explain the process of their construction, making clear how and why we have chosen the stories we focus on and encouraging the audience to challenge them. We are, of course, historically situated too. We are here, now, and this place is only manifesting as it is because of the foundations it builds on. Some of the neoliberal processes we are opposed to, such as marketisation and privatisation, seem impossible to stop, and often there is a sense that all we can do is bear witness. However, an understanding of history makes clear there is nothing natural about capitalism and we can also take heart from stories of community. I hope also we can imagine a different future and take steps towards making that a reality too.

**CR**: Movement sometimes becomes implicated with progress – perhaps we have become so conditioned to an 'onward and upward' mentality that it is hard to think of it as cyclical or patterned or arbitrary. We are either going up or coming down, forwards or backwards, stuck in some binary track. How do you see it?

**MR**: Certainly not as linear, inevitable or inevitably positive. There is something fundamentally flawed in equating progress with ideas of economic growth in a world of finite resources and growing inequality. This also suggests we are the pinnacle of achievement and that is a stifling, disturbing thought. As I've mentioned before, a critique of regeneration and development narratives is really integral to all my work. However, I also want to avoid nostalgia; I certainly don't believe in a mythical golden age to which we can, or should, return. Personally, without modern healthcare and technologies I wouldn't be here, so this is literally the only time I could be alive. I have a fear that eugenics may make that even more resonant, but that's another conversation.

I seldom find binaries a useful way of thinking about anything; a spectrum better reflects most situations, although that probably doesn't work for time – I'm not a physicist or a Time Lord, so I can only grasp at analogies to try and explain my perspective. In some ways, the palimpsest remains a useful metaphor for how I think time affects space: a constant layering and rewriting on top of what went before. However, the layers are permeable and the past leaks through; some layers are thicker than others. In places we are overwhelmed by the weight of history and in others it has almost been erased…

I like Mark Fisher's writing on hauntology (2014), where he examines popular culture and its tendency to recycle and re-appropriate the past, creating feelings of dislocation and despair. Fisher links this to what he calls 'Capitalist Realism' – a collective mental state where we can't see a way through or beyond marketisation, where even our imaginations have been colonised. We are nostalgic for a time when there were collective visions of a brighter future and this results in a sense of time that has blurred and fluid boundaries. The half-remembered dreams of an imagined Utopia we may experience are perhaps akin to moments of authentic desire that may be glimpsed through gaps in Debord's spectacle.

Thinking about your interest in psychoanalysis, the work of Steve Pile is also relevant. He explores how the emotional, mental and dream work of cities is as important as other more material forms of producing space. In Real Cities (Pile, 2005), he talks about the character of specific locations and how they can be associated with the construction and significance of dreams, magic, ghosts and vampires. Pile suggests a psychogeographical analysis can be useful to understanding places because it goes 'beyond the surface appearance of things'. The mythical and supernatural linger in the contemporary secular city, haunting us not literally but through the city's subconscious. We may use a different conceptual framework to articulate this, but I can see common ground here.

Examining the stories Manchester tells itself, uncovering those that are hidden and valuing a multiplicity of voices are all absolutely key to the LRM. Those tales are all around us, beneath our feet, in our imaginations, waiting to become manifest through wandering. Perhaps, by walking together, we will create new narratives that can shape the city we dream of. At the very least, the journey will give our maps a brighter, broader perspective when we redesign them according to our shared experiences and realise the lines are an illusion. We have the power to redraw our worlds and erase borders.

**CR**: The idea of making our own maps links with the writing I've been doing about mapmaking in psychotherapy. It's been a fascinating conversation, with a lot of resonances for me. Before we finish, I want to ask what drew you into this, and what sustains you?

**MR**: Initially it was an emotional and visceral drawing in. I was angry at what I could see happening to the city – the erosion of public space, homogenisation and gentrification, the slow violence of neoliberalism. I was also in love with the street and hungry to learn more. I previously mentioned The Basement as a catalyst and inspiration, where we worked collectively to provide a non-commercial hub in the city. Our DIY ethos built a space to share ideas and for activists to conspire and cross-pollinate. [There are other social centres and radical bookshops across the country and I urge you to support them. The Basement itself was closed following a fire in 2008.] The Basement gave me the opportunity to develop a fledging interest in psychogeography in a supportive environment, and I am so grateful to them.

At the same time, I had some issues with a definition of activism that could be exclusionary and disconnected from many people. My day job was in community development and I met many people who were doing amazing things within their neighbourhoods but didn't always have the space to engage with political theory. I wanted to find a way to bridge that gap, to bring politics and theory onto the street and to start conversations between different groups who all wanted to make Manchester better and more interesting, and perhaps expand what we value as activism. Also, importantly, I wanted to have fun and make space for play.

The first LRM events didn't use a group name; they were 'May Day *Dérives*' or explorations of what psychogeography could mean. It sort of escalated from there, and the group has wandered and wondered together ever since. What sustains me now is not really so different; there is always something new to see and learn, and I am still walking through my fascination with and ambivalent relationship to Manchester. Plus, I am stubborn and all those issues of social and spatial justice are still unresolved.

## References

Benjamin W (1999). *The Arcades Project*. Cambridge, MA: Harvard University Press.

Debord G (1967/1992). *The Society of the Spectacle* (Knabb K, trans). London: Rebel Press.

Debord G (1955). Introduction to a critique of urban geography. In: Knabb K (ed & trans). *Situationist International Anthology* (revised and expanded edition). Berkeley, CA: Bureau of Public Secrets (pp8–12).

Fisher M (2014). *Ghosts of my Life: writings on depression, hauntology and lost futures*. Winchester: Zero Books.

Fulton H (undated). [Online.] www.hamish-fulton.com/quotes.txt (accessed 20 November 2018).

Massey D (2005). *For Space*. London: Sage.

Pile S (2005). *Real Cities: modernity, space and the phantasmagorias of city life*. London: Sage.

Richardson T (ed) (2015). *Walking Inside Out: contemporary British psychogeography*. London: Rowman and Littlefield.

Smith P (2010). *Mythogeography: a guide to walking sideways*. Charmouth: Triarchy Press.

Vaneigem R (1967). *The Revolution of Everyday Life* (Nicholson-Smith D, trans). Oakland, CA: PM Press.

# 7 | The theory and practice of urban therapy
## Phil Wood

> How we imagine our cities, how we envision their goals and values and enhance their beauty defines the self of each person in that city, for the city is the solid exhibition of the communal soul. This means that you find yourself by entering the crowd – which is the root meaning of the word polis – poly – flow and many. To improve yourself you improve your city. This idea is so intolerable to the individualized Self that prefers delusions of calm isolation and meditative retreat as the road to Self, I am suggesting. Self is the actual road, the city street.
> James Hillman, *City and Soul* (2006: 115)

We live in a society of unprecedented complexity and inter-connectedness, and nothing characterises this better than the city. While we humans have walked the Earth for about 250,000 years, we have only been living in urban communities that bear any resemblance to today's cities for a couple of centuries at most. You could say that we are still learners in the business of city dwelling, yet more than half of us now do it.

The city is the greatest threat to our place on this planet, through its propensity to generate pollution, pestilence, conflict and economic collapse, and often places an unbearable physical and psychic pressure upon us as individuals. But the city is also where humankind can find the greatest resilience and the solutions it needs to overcome these threats and to thrive.

Urban therapy is a way of thinking about and working with the human-built and natural environment. It sees the city as a complex adaptive system, where an understanding of individual parts does not automatically convey knowledge of the behaviour of the whole – thus requiring a holistic, interdisciplinary and intercultural approach. Adopting metaphors from biology and psychology, it understands physical places and settlements as organic and sentient. It rejects pathologising cities as a sickness to be cured, preferring the nurturing of wellbeing and preventative care as its modus operandi.

As an urban therapist, I usually work in places that are anticipating, undergoing or recovering from change or trauma, and in a multidisciplinary team with place-making professionals, social and community workers, political scientists, artists and residents. The ultimate outcome may be a physical entity, a plan or a programme of work, but the process of diverse people learning and acting together is often the most significant element. Common techniques of the urban therapist include psychogeographic walking and mapping, story-telling and artistic envisioning and metaphor. This chapter looks at some of the key historical and intellectual influences, before discussing a selection of the experiences and projects that I have admired or been associated with.

## The city and the mind

Both Renaissance and Enlightenment thinkers were concerned with the idea of the good city, derived from Plato, that could be shaped and would in turn shape us to live virtuously. This utopian tradition lives on into the present day, but it might best be exemplified by the experiments of the 19th century: Titus Salt's paternalistic model village of Saltaire, shading into the more socially liberal with Cadbury's Bournville and Ebenezer Howard's Garden City movement (Howard, 1902).

The most seminal role, however, was played by Patrick Geddes (1915/1949). Credited with being the founder of the town planning profession, the influence of Charles Darwin gave him an understanding of the city as an evolutionary, reflexive and responsive entity (Batty & Marshall, 2017). The idea of the city as a complex self-adaptive system first emerged with Geddes and we now find parallels in latter-day understandings of the human brain (with the emergence of neuroplasticity), which have not been lost on contemporary urban theorists (Sullivan, 2018).

We can trace the influence of Geddes on the Chicago School of urbanists, when Robert Park and Ernest Burgess wrote that 'the city is not merely a physical mechanism and an artificial construction. It is involved in the vital processes of the people who compose it' (Park, Burgess & McKenzie, 1925/1984: 1). Jane Jacobs (1961) and Herbert Gans (1962) picked up these ideas in the context of the vast programmes of demolition and redevelopment that were being imposed on American and European cities to accommodate the motor car, systems building and property speculation, and the grievous effects these were having on communities. Peter Marris (1974) went further still, making an explicit connection between urban policy and psychological wellbeing, with reference to people losing their homes. Marie Jahoda (1982), influenced by Freud, also began studying communities traumatised by mass unemployment from a psychosocial perspective.

It is the work of Leonie Sandercock that has drawn these various threads together into a deliberate melding of the urbanist, psychological and community development literature to produce the notion of therapeutic planning (2004), and it is through reading and working with Sandercock that my own thinking has crystallised as urban therapy.

Sandercock is interested in the growing number of situations in our intensely diverse and complex cities where an abstract and detached approach to urban planning and decision-making is not only no longer relevant but potentially damaging. She demands:

> … recognition of the need for a language and a process of emotional involvement, of embodiment. This means not only allowing the 'whole person' to be present in negotiations and deliberations but being prepared to acknowledge and deal with the powerful emotions that underpin many planning issues… what I am calling a 'therapeutic' approach is the possibility of transformation… Just as in successful therapy there is breakthrough and individual growth becomes possible, so too, with a successful therapeutically oriented approach to managing

our coexistence in the shared spaces of neighbourhoods, cities
and regions, there is the capacity for collective growth. (2004: 139)

Others have recounted practical examples of how this therapeutic
planning may be operationalised. Erfan (2016) describes work
with indigenous communities to undo years of damaging
rationalist planning and psychology imposed from above, while
Gunder and Hillier (2007) describe experiments from Australia
and New Zealand, and Umemoto (2001) explores the challenges
of crossing cultural and linguistic boundaries. Meanwhile,
Schweitzer (2016) argues that it may never be possible to
rescue therapy from the one-sided counsellor-patient power
relationship, and so she seeks other metaphors from psychology,
such as restorative care and justice.

Georg Simmel, in his classic essay 'The Metropolis and
Mental Life' (1905/1950), asked: 'What impact has the rapidly
changing urban environment on our inner life?' His answer hinges
on his concept of 'the intensification of nervous stimulation'
once we move from the bucolic village to the bustling city. He
identified a new urban mentality that insulated itself from the
daily challenges of urban life with a blasé detachment and a
heightened rationality.

One of Simmel's students was Walter Benjamin, who is now
fêted as a fundamental precursor of psychogeography. In *The
Arcades Project* (1999), Benjamin propounds two complementary
concepts to explain our human response to modern city life.
*Erlebnis* (lived experience) can be characterised as the shock-
induced anaesthesia brought about by the overwhelming sensory
bombardment of life in a modern city. *Erfahrung* (wisdom
drawn from experience) is a more positive response and refers
to the aimless sauntering of the *flâneur* and the unmediated
appreciation of the wealth of sights, sounds and smells the city
has to offer. Benjamin was particularly interested in the creative
possibilities of the dialectic between these two concepts. This
critical, non-functionalist and deconstructive approach to
the urban mind can be seen to have fed into the work of the
Situationist International and key figures of psychogeography
such as Iain Sinclair.

But seven decades had to pass before a professional psychologist took serious account of Simmel's work. Stanley Milgram is best known for his controversial experiments with obedience, but the majority of his work focused on city living. His book *The Experience of Living in Cities* (1970) was the first expression of what became known as urban psychology. Milgram went beyond Simmel's sociological analysis to adapt the concept of stimulus overload from cybernetics, linking the urban environment with individual experience. He based his work on data produced by field experimentation and other empirical methods, aiming for an objective, non-judgemental description of urban life, which contrasted with the negative urbanology of the time that saw the city as a tangle of (potentially insoluble) problems (Blass, 1992).

It was Henri Lefebvre who best summarised, and parodied, this persistent trope in both psychology and urbanism to medicalise and pathologise people and places:

> Planning as ideology formulates all the problems of society
> into questions of space… what are represented are healthy
> and diseased spaces. The planner should be able to distinguish
> between sick spaces and spaces linked to mental and social
> health which are generators of this health. As physicians of space,
> he [sic] should have the capacity to conceive of an harmonious
> social space, normal and normalizing. (Lefebvre, 1996: 99)

A further development has been the emergence of a geographical psychology dedicated to 'discover and understand the spatial organisation of psychological phenomena and how that organisation relates to individual behaviour and the macro environment' (Rentfrow & Jokela, 2016: 393). Could it be demonstrated that different characteristics or behaviours were associated with different locales, and could it be deduced from this that a city has its own personality? Is it possible to say that some cities or neighbourhoods are more sociable, open and curious or more aggressive than others? If so, could this be attributable to social influence: that is, to the effects of actions within the local environment on an individual's own thoughts? Could it be an ecological influence, whereby the climate, terrain, built environment or population density impact a person's psyche, or the result of selective migration, whereby people imperceptibly cluster to be closer to people who reinforce their psychological needs (Gallagher, 1993)? Or, most likely, is it an interplay of all these factors? These ideas have been taken up by, among others, James Hillman (2006), Thomas Singer (2010) and Charles Landry (Landry & Murray, 2017).

## Therapy for the city

However, thinking of personality as characteristic and habitual ways of behaving and feeling, rather than as fixed and enduring traits, opens up the possibility of adaptation and healing. Places, like people, can be subject to varying forms and degrees of detriment and hurt. There is the traumatic physical damage of natural catastrophe, conflict or planned demolition, as well as the imperceptible creep into neglect and decay. And there are psychic equivalents too: say, the demonising of a place for its association with a heinous event or idea, the faultlines of sectarian division, or the feeling of being stuck in the past or lacking a sense of future purpose.

Therapy for the city may incorporate a range of approaches. It might involve the creation of a special space of sanctuary, within but away from the stress of the city, in which therapeutic processes and encounters may occur.[1] Or it could involve the creation of common-purpose initiatives to restore physical degradation, to mediate current disagreements or to work through unresolved memories or collective subconscious trauma. But it also incorporates the way of thinking about the city as an entity that, if cared for, will itself become a reciprocal source of healing and wellbeing for its citizens, thus moving beyond the counsellor/patient metaphor.[2]

Given that the city is a dynamic environment, based on the interplay of interest groups and power structures, the healing must also take into account the threat of relapse or recurrence of the problematic symptoms. Thus, to achieve true healing there may be

---

1. For example, I have been associated with the creation of a 'Garden of Reflection' in Derry/Londonderry, Northern Ireland.

2. This is the practice of 'milieu therapy' explored by Fullilove (2013) in relation to the aftermath of 9/11 in New York.

the need for symbolic and actual change, including the remedy of past wrongs, collective or institutional compensation or restitution, or enacted reform that brings institutions into line with the values that emerge from the healing process (Schweitzer, 2016).

Urban therapy has also always had a concern with diversity (both of the human mind and society) and a conviction that this is not a problem to be solved but an opportunity to be realised. Gordon Allport's (1954) pioneering contact hypothesis argued that, under appropriate conditions, interpersonal contact is one of the most effective ways to reduce prejudice between majority and minority group members. This became a foundational idea in my own book, *The Intercultural City* (Wood & Landry, 2008), which argues that cities with a psychological openness to difference and uncertainty will thrive under contemporary conditions of super-diversity and rapid, unpredictable change.

I will now turn to some examples of work that I have either observed or participated in and that encapsulate aspects of urban therapy as I conceive it. For reasons of economy of space and coherence of purpose, I have limited myself to examples that involve groups or individuals moving through urban space, holding closely to the emphasis on walking and psychogeography in this book.

## Planning For Real

The first is a seminal experience in my first job as a community development worker in my home town, after a rapid economic downturn led to mass unemployment and what I came to understand as symptoms of collective trauma. I had been talking for months to people on one very large housing estate, and was struck by their sense of impotence and inability to make any change or improvement to their lives or the place they lived in. I had tried to involve the town council's psychological and social work department but found it uninterested beyond its model of one-to-one casework.[3] At the other extreme, the housing

3. Worryingly, there appears to have been little progress in three decades, with the journal *Child and Family Social Work* recently noting that '... apart from one or two isolated examples... there is virtually no consideration in the social work literature, or in practice, of the meanings of place to children and adults, and its influences on their behaviour and well-being' (Jack, 2015).

and planning departments saw the world in terms of units and maps and were deeply suspicious of anything that might arouse individual or collective agency in the residents.

I became aware of Planning For Real, a liberating methodology devised by a remarkable activist, Dr Tony Gibson, who ran Education for Neighbourhood Change (Gibson, 1991). It was a process in which local people would walk around and collectively analyse their neighbourhood (its assets, liabilities, stories and power relationships),[4] create a giant-scale map and model of it, then get on their hands and knees with various professionals and use the map and model to make plans for improvement, then finally do more walks to refine and embed their ideas.

I invited Gibson to work with us, and his ideas and personality enlivened people, particularly because it encouraged them to physically explore and encompass their space and collectively discover things about it, and themselves, that they habitually overlooked or undervalued. The residents took to heart this walking and mapping technique and repeated it in many variations over a long process of revival that eventually saw the estate fêted as a model community.

This was a formative experience for me in a number of ways. First, it showed me that places and not just people have personalities and moods and are responsive to a therapeutic approach. Second, it demonstrated that, even in conditions of extreme individual and collective misfortune, some powerful and quite magical things can start to happen when people get to their feet and walk as a group in a space (Oppezzo & Schwartz, 2014). Third, it showed that professional demarcations had no answers to the complex collective issues I was encountering, and that more holistic approaches were needed. And, finally, I realised I no longer needed to agonise over whether I should pigeonhole myself as a community worker, social worker, planner or whatever, and that I could give myself permission to invent the new hybrid profession of 'urban therapist'.

4. This was something Gibson described as 'transect walking', see www.planningforreal. org.uk/what-is-pfr/our-other-techniques (accessed 5 April 2019).

## Birmingham

A few years ago, my colleague Charles Landry and I were invited by Birmingham City Council to offer a different slant on how it could rethink the direction the city should be taking in a post-industrial environment. We arranged a three-day event (known as Highbury 3) to which we invited an extremely diverse cross-section of 150 of the city's activists and opinion leaders and invited them to think audacious thoughts. The challenge was to get them out into the city in ways that would enable them to turn dry, abstract concepts like cohesion, connectivity or culture into live issues.

Twelve groups set out to explore different topics but the one that particularly caught my imagination took the public bus to the deprived neighbourhood of Small Heath to think about physical and mental wellbeing. The group leader, Jackie Chambers (a public health professional), believed the best way of learning was experiential, so, when they arrived in Small Heath, she told her group they would be role-playing the lives of ordinary residents. They were relieved of their mobile phones and credit cards and given a small cash allowance and a set of assignments. These included assuming a new identity and, where appropriate, props that would help them experience that identity: for example, a pushchair with a crying baby doll, a heavy apron (to simulate obesity), a wheelchair, heavy glasses or a hearing aid. They were then instructed to walk through the local park and along the main shopping street to try to assemble ingredients for a healthy family meal, before finally trying to negotiate their way back to the city centre on what was left of their meagre allowance.

We can be sure that barely anyone in the group had done such things in decades, if at all, and the effect on them was profound. I still recall the looks of shock and awe on their faces as they straggled back into Birmingham's International Convention Centre after an experience none would forget in a hurry. In a true psychogeographical sense, this experience fundamentally altered the way local powerbrokers would think about the city they thought they knew.

## Rotterdam

I experienced another example, in a similar vein, in the Dutch city of Rotterdam. I enrolled on a City Safari, which offered me a voluminous list of local residents and institutions that would willingly open their door to a stranger and give me a one-hour insight into their lives, from which I was invited to select an itinerary of four. The organisers made the introductions and suggested a route to walk between my destinations through different districts of the city. I chose to visit a Surinamese mosque, the kitchen of an Antillian community activist, a recent Nigerian migrant, and two Dutch pensioners who had lived in the same house since the Second World War.

I found the experience of walking through unknown parts of the city and knocking on strange doors gave me a heightened sense of awareness of Rotterdam and also of my own ability to interact with people in radically different situations. But, strictly speaking, City Safari is not aimed at people like me at all, but at Rotterdammers themselves. I've since got to know the organisers, Marjolijn Masselink and Kees de Gruiter, and their message is 'Be a tourist in your own city' but also 'Debunk the fears and prejudices you hold about your fellow citizens and the places in which they live'.

Marjolijn and Kees acknowledge the squeamishness with which liberal opinion may regard the use of the word 'safari' in such a context, but in Swahili it means 'my journey', which perfectly captures the process of self- and place-discovery beyond one's comfort zone. They are also keen to assert that City Safari is a business that charges a fee and makes a profit, which is then shared between the hosts and organisers, and they don't consider themselves as either therapists or do-gooders.

Nevertheless, they are aware of the good that they do. Shortly before our interview, they had organised walking itineraries for 120 of the city's professional social workers, all of whom thought they knew the city their clients live in but were amazed to find that they didn't. They also told me about one of their hosts, an Afghan refugee, who had agreed to open her doors to visitors after a long period of isolation. She said she felt so empowered by the idea of people walking across the city to receive her hospitality and hear her story that she took the momentous decision to abandon her identity as a refugee and adopt a new one as an *Echte* (real) *Rotterdammer*.

Kees told me: 'When you step out of a station or a hotel into a strange city, you can either take a right in the direction of the souvenir stall, or take a left into the unknown.' He also remarked that: 'I always sit down, watch and ask myself, why do people do this and not that? Once you've figured out why people use one side of the street but not the other, you're already beginning to fathom that city. Without a deep understanding of the complex organism that the city is, you can't begin to improve it.'

Kees has now taken the City Safari approach elsewhere, including Athens, Nairobi and Philadelphia. He sees them all as cities that, like Rotterdam, are segmented by ethnic and class segregation, which he hopes his work might mitigate. But there are also some cities where the divisions are so visible and palpable that they are an open wound that will not heal – which brings me to my next example.

## Mostar

I have visited many divided cities – Jerusalem, Johannesburg, Belfast and Nicosia – where past or present struggles leave a legacy of physical and social separation, but there is something more visceral about Mostar in Bosnia-Herzegovina. The Neretva River runs through a deep gorge that separates the city into two halves. It is bridged by the iconic Stari Most (Old Bridge), which was destroyed during the Croat-Bosniak War in 1993 and rebuilt 11 years later, to great acclaim. Sadly, the physical reconnection of the two banks was not enough to bridge the political and cultural divide between Catholic Croats and Muslim Bosniaks, which festers on, more than two decades after the war. While there is an absence of conflict and the veneer of a normally functioning city, Mostar and almost all its institutions are divided, with the river acting as the frontier (Bollens, 2012).

When I visited Mostar, I was the guest of one of the handful of public entities that defy the culture of apartheid and expressly reach out to all ethnic communities, the OKC (Youth Cultural

Centre) Abrašević. While there, I participated in a walk across the city led by one of the centre's founders, Ronald Panza, which left a deep impression on me.

It was originally founded during the Yugoslavian times as RKUD (Workers' Cultural-Artistic Society) Abrašević, named for a famous poet, where folk music was played and people gathered after working hours. The centre's premises were almost completely destroyed during the Yugoslav Wars, but a group of local activists and artists reclaimed the ruins to make a space to provide young people with creative opportunities and nurture intellectual freedom (Carabelli, 2013).

While music, dance and art are the daily staples of the centre, Ronald believes that, in a city in which public space has become so ethnically demarcated and politicised, walking has an important part to play. He led me along a series of twists and turns, along alleyways and narrow streets, past cemeteries and through squares, until I almost lost my bearings. Much of the city remains in ruins, with gaunt, gutted structures at every turn, although the restored Stari Most offers a vision of what a revived Mostar might become.

Ronald knew intimately every step we were taking, but he was not behaving as a conventional tour guide. He fed us minimal information about the spaces we passed through, allowing our own imaginations to construct an image of what may have happened there, or what ghosts still haunted them. Our walk concluded on a hill overlooking the city, the site of the profoundly evocative Partisan Memorial, designed by the great humanist Bogdan Bogdanović, a figure who represents a powerful alternative to the decades of strife and bigotry that have beset Bosnia-Herzegovina.

I have written elsewhere about this remarkable monument;[5] here I want to mark the courage and foresight of Ronald Panza in making himself a visible pedestrian symbol of what this city was, is and could become. In a more elaborated version of the walk I participated in, Ronald designed a documentary audio story, *From Us To The City*, about the building and the urban quarter surrounding it. Walkers were invited to put on headphones and

5. See http://subversiveurbanism.tumblr.com/post/22802654170/a-transcendental-alternative-to-balkan-reality (accessed 7 April 2019).

move through a series of locations where they heard the stories of places that were gone or stand in ruins, as well as the concepts behind places and democratic institutions that were planned but never built. Ronald wished to remind his damaged, sleep-walking city that Abrašević represents a time when Mostar was a symbol of multi-ethnic harmony and creativity.[6]

## Lisbon

Nadia Sacoor is a Londoner of mixed Indian and European heritage who settled in Lisbon to work with the Aga Khan Foundation on its K'Cidade community development programme. She is a trained psychologist who is fascinated with the possibilities of intercultural mixing.

Walking the streets of the inner-city district of Mouraria, Nadia had the revelation that a district could be understood not only by people who were visibly present but also by those who were not visible. In this case, she meant the women of immigrant households who remained confined to the home, whether for reasons of cultural constraint, lack of language or fear of the unknown. In particular, there are many Bangladeshi, Nepali and Chinese residents in the district and, while the menfolk are conspicuous in the restaurants and open-all-hours shops, the girls and women are rarely to be seen, Nadia realised. After months of persistence, she managed to gain the confidence of a few women, with whom she was able to develop trusting relationships. She began to make up a map of her movements and encounters so she could start to understand patterns of behaviour, and along the way she was getting herself recognised and trusted in the neighbourhood.

With time, she was able to exchange words with certain women and some would even agree to share a cup of tea in a café. None would respond to direct questioning about their lifestyle but, at their own pace, some would slowly divulge their stories. It became clear to Nadia that not all the women she met were entirely happy with their housebound status and that, for some,

---

6. One participant in the walk has written a touching photo-blog of her experience. See http://amostarradiography.org/what-would-kosta-say-now (accessed 5 April 2019).

it was a stressful and psychologically difficult lifestyle. Through her mapping, she was able to build up a clear pattern of the places where the women did, or would, feel comfortable, and she suggested informal gatherings in tea shops. After this, it was a natural progression to start walking between these 'safe zones' and soon it was the women, rather than Nadia, who were suggesting the routes to be followed.

All the time, Nadia was careful to avoid directing the group and to allow the walking routes to develop organically as the growing group of women became more confident and added more locations to their repertoire. Then came the revelation that these group walks were starting to become a noticeable feature of Mouraria's street life. Locals were becoming aware for the first time that they were sharing their streets with people with exotic dress and demeanour. 'None of the women see it as an overtly political act,' says Nadia, 'but I can see that, in their discrete occupation of space, this is an important step for Lisbon.' For the women, Nadia thinks the impact is far more personal, and to do with their own psychological resilience to successfully adapt to life in the face of adversity. Stress, whether in the form of family or relationship problems or health or financial worries, that previously might have been locked up in the household or their own heads, now has a wider context in which these difficulties might be resolved.

## Huddersfield

There are some occasions when a walk can become a performance in space, and this can have its own very special therapeutic resonance. I discovered this while co-organising a festival in my home town, which we immodestly entitled the 'Fourth World Congress of Psychogeography'. We had received an intriguing proposal for a street performance from a San Francisco-based Spanish artist, Elia Rita.

She offered her piece *I'm the City of Others Who Are the City* as an 'urban pilgrimage', to be performed in a busy Huddersfield shopping precinct on a Saturday afternoon 'as an act of worship to the urban landscape and its inhabitants, turning it into a sacred site for a short period of time'. She explained that 'the simple act of walking is chosen for its ability to be a non-violent method of reclamation and activation of public space: space that confirms our individual and shared identities'.

I wasn't sure that my northern English mill town was quite ready to have its main street turned into a sacred site. On a Saturday afternoon, King Street can be a brisk and even intimidating place of head-down, no-nonsense shoppers and lairy drinkers.

Elia arrived wearing flowing white robes and, without any announcement, began her ritual. It comprised just five movements: standing upright, a forward bow, lying on the ground with upper body raised on extended arms and then a full prostration, followed by a return to the upright and a step forward, all conducted in total silence. With this she set out to cover a distance of about 100 metres in two hours. The surface was hard and wet and the weather cold and blustery – more Pennine than Californian. I stood back and observed. What happened next enchanted me.

People were hurriedly passing by, and then a few actually stopped in their tracks, intrigued by the unprecedented spectacle in their street. They were inured to being importuned by buskers, chuggers and opinion surveyors, but this diminutive woman in white seemed to want nothing from them. Curious, people started looking around for someone who might be in charge to find out what was going on. They turned to each other and, in the absence of any explanation, began formulating their own theories: 'I've heard she's on a pilgrimage.' 'Yeah, but where to?' 'Who is she worshipping?' 'Does it matter? I just like it.'

A crowd was gathering now. One well-known local street drinker faced Elia and asked her directly what she thought she was up to. I intervened very gently and explained she was enacting a ritual about transcending the pain she was putting herself through. 'Ohh, now I get it. I know all about pain, me. I'm riddled with cancer. Do you think she might – you know – lay her hands on me?'

As my anxiety receded and I started adjusting to the pace of Elia's movement, I realised something quite magical was happening in the street. The ambient noise level had appreciably fallen and people who were still talking had adopted hushed tones. Many had now stopped and even those who walked through seemed to be moving at a respectfully slower pace. A group of teenage girls who had tumbled noisily out of a shop into the middle of the spectacle had abandoned their Snapchat messaging and were whispering to each other. I joined in the conversation: 'This is amazing. I really respect her for doing this'; 'I know, I feel so calm. I wish I could join in.'

One quite elderly woman didn't wait to be asked. She knelt down beside Elia and mirrored her movements. I spoke to her afterwards and she told me she had simply been passing through King Street on the way home from visiting a friend who had just tragically lost a relative to cancer. She said she had seen Elia and, without thinking, had simply felt at one with her. Joining her pilgrimage had given her a chance momentarily to clear her mind of the turmoil within. She couldn't thank Elia enough.

We were almost at the end of the street when a homeless man stood directly in front of Elia. He placed his beer can carefully on the flagstones and then prostrated himself in front of her. He then stood, retrieved his drink and moved on. And then it was all over, and King Street returned to normal.

I talked to Elia afterwards about where she found the psychic and physical strength to carry out a piece like this in what for her must have been such an alien environment. She told me Eastern spiritual practices have informed her performance but she has broadened them to become aesthetic and political. As an artist, she rejects traditional art spaces in preference to the open air in the belief that her work will be shared with a wider public, bringing awareness of the loss of common space and the accelerated pace of living that individualises and distances us from our communal selves.

## Conclusion

In this chapter, I have tried to make the case that places and groups, and not just individuals, have personality, spirit and soul. They are equally susceptible to strain, abuse and trauma and respond benignly to a practice of care and therapy – and the 'consulting room' for this practice can be a walk in the street. I have spent most of my career working with place-making professionals, politicians and individuals as citizen activists, encouraging them to find space for matters of the psyche and soul in urban affairs. Here I hope to have made a case that all individuals are naturally engaged in a dynamic interaction between their inner psyche and outer environment, and to have stimulated some curiosity to explore further the implications of this. The prevailing trope that the city is a man-made pathology to be resisted or avoided is ultimately a counsel of despair. If we can instead understand the city as a complex, adaptive, thinking, feeling entity – like ourselves – then maybe we can fashion a mutuality of purpose in which both can psychically grow and thrive together.

## References

Allport G (1954). *The Nature of Prejudice*. Reading, MA: Addison-Wesley.

Batty M, Marshall S (2017). Thinking organic, acting civic: the paradox of planning for cities in evolution. *Landscape and Urban Planning 166*: 4–14.

Benjamin W (1999). *The Arcades Project*. Cambridge, MA: Harvard University Press.

Blass T (1992). The social psychology of Stanley Milgram. *Advances in Experimental Social Psychology 25*: 277–329.

Bollens S (2012). *City and Soul in Divided Societies*. London: Routledge.

Carabelli G (2013). Living (critically) in the present: youth activism in Mostar (Bosnia Herzegovina). *European Perspectives – Journal on European Perspectives of the Western Balkans 5*(1): 50–67.

Erfan A (2016). Confronting collective traumas: an exploration of therapeutic planning. *Planning Theory & Practice 18*(1): 34–50.

Fullilove M (2013). *Urban Alchemy: restoring joy in America's sorted-out cities*. New York, NY: New Village Press.

Gallagher W (1993). *The Power of Place: how our surroundings shape our thoughts, emotions, and actions*. New York, NY: Simon & Schuster.

Gans H (1962). *Urban Villagers*. New York, NY: Simon and Schuster.

Geddes P (1915/1949). *Cities in Evolution* (new and revised ed). London: William and Norgate.

Gibson T (1991). Planning for real: the approach of the Neighbourhood Initiatives Foundation in the UK. *RRA Notes 11*: 29–30.

Gunder M, Hillier J (2007). Planning as urban therapeutic. *Environment and Planning A 39*(2): 467–486.

Hillman J (2006). *City and Soul: uniform edition* (vol 2). Thompson, CT: Spring Publications.

Howard E (1902). *Garden Cities of Tomorrow* (original 1898 title: *Tomorrow: a peaceful path to real reform*). London: S Sonnenschein & Co.

Jack G (2015). 'I may not know who I am, but I know where I am from': the meaning of place in social work with children and families. *Child & Family Social Work 20*(4): 415–423.

Jacobs J (1961). *The Death and Life of Great American Cities.* New York, NY: Vintage.

Jahoda M (1982). *Employment and Unemployment: a social-psychological analysis.* Cambridge: Cambridge University Press.

Landry C, Murray C (2017). *Psychology and the City: the hidden dimension.* Bournes Green: Comedia.

Lefebvre H (1996). *Writings on Cities* (E Kofman, E Lebas, eds & trans). London: Blackwell.

Marris P (1974). *Loss and Change.* London: Routledge.

Milgram S (1970). The experience of living in cities. *Science 167*(3924): 1461–1468.

Oppezzo M, Schwartz D (2014). Give your ideas some legs: the positive effect of walking on creative thinking. *Journal of Experimental Psychology: Learning, Memory, and Cognition 40*(4): 1142.

Park R, Burgess E, McKenzie RD (1925/1984). *The City.* Chicago, IL: University of Chicago Press.

Rentfrow P, Jokela M (2016). Geographical psychology: the spatial organization of psychological phenomena. *Current Directions in Psychological Science 25*(6): 393–398.

Sandercock L (2004). Towards a planning imagination for the 21st century. *Journal of the American Planning Association 70*(2): 133–141.

Schweitzer L (2016). Restorative planning ethics: the therapeutic imagination and planning in public institutions. *Planning Theory 15*(2): 130–144.

Simmel G (1905/1950). The metropolis and mental life. In: Simmel G. *The Sociology of Georg Simmel.* New York, NY: Simon & Schuster.

Singer T (ed). (2010). *Psyche and the City: a soul's guide to the modern metropolis.* New Orleans, LA: Spring Journal Books.

Sullivan R (2018). *Twenty-First Century Urbanism: a new analysis of the city.* London: Routledge.

Umemoto K (2001). Walking in another's shoes: epistemological challenges in participatory planning. *Journal of Planning Education and Research 21*(1): 17–31.

Wood P, Landry C (2008). *The Intercultural City: planning for diversity advantage.* London: Routledge.

# 8 | 'Here' is where I have a presence
## Karen Izod

*I recognise this place, its air saturated*
*With the echo-waves of a spent force ten.*

From 'Gollan Head: former home to RAF radar station, Outer
Hebrides' (Izod, 2017: 36)

I wrote these opening lines to my poem 'Gollan Head' (Izod,
2017: 36) in response to a visit to this wonder-full place at the
extreme western edge of the Isle of Lewis. Open to a wild Atlantic,
this former RAF radar station still held a turbulence in the air
from recent gales and the echoes of its past. I had never been there
before, yet it registered with me as somewhere recognisable. It was
a familiar place.

There was much that I could associate with: a familiar sense
of being scared on high cliffs in high wind, the abandoned RAF
station that was being brought back to life, with its curious
combination of desolation and hope, and the fulmars holding
tightly to their chinks in the rock faces below. All these things
made an impression on me in a way that said, 'I know this place.
It offers an example of a place where my own inner landscape, a
world of thoughts, feelings, imaginings, is laid out and becomes
visible. It offers a landscape that, should I choose, I can work with
to explore my inner world.'

Two years later I went back. It was a fine day, with a low wind;
the windows in the former RAF accommodation looked less bare;

the place altogether more settled. I could connect to the agitation I felt on the first occasion but it had lessened. It suggested to me that the changes were not only in this immediate environment but that my own response to it had shifted too.

## This landscape…

My intention in this chapter is to create a landscape of a kind where you can find places that evoke a line of thinking, resonate with particular memories and bring forth an array of emotions. You may stumble upon pieces that stimulate your curiosity and imagination and pieces that you may pass by or find yourself returning to. It is a meander, incomplete, as an essay of this kind inevitably is. It attempts a journey between descriptions of places, reflections on loss and change and deliberations on attachment and meaning-making, and brings attention to the nature of recognition – of place, and one's own place within it.

## Orientation and perspective…

I live on the edges of the North Downs in Merrow, Surrey – altogether a different place to Gollan Head, with its soft and rolling chalk grasslands and remains of flint quarries. At this time of year (September 2017), it is covered with wild chamomile, yarrow and creeping thistle; the hedgerows are thick with sloes and the brambles are beginning to die away. At the top of the expanse of grassland known as Brownings Down is a 180° vista: the simple splendour of Guildford Cathedral, its angel flaming in the west, through to the distant and distinctive Canary Wharf in the east. It is a place of orientation, of knowing where I am, and I can locate myself in relation to others within what is probably a 40-mile horizon. Nearby, at Newlands Corner, the views are even more extensive. Looking to the south, over the receding Surrey Hills, I am always reminded of Gerard Manley Hopkins' idea of 'inscape' – the essence that gives each thing its uniqueness. I associate it with an unfolding: that the landscape unfolds and reveals itself to itself.

When I was a practising social worker in the 1970s and 1980s, I would come here with some of the children and young adults I was working with, to play, walk, talk, or just let something about this place make itself felt. The sense of possibility – '*I feel like I'm flying*' – or of perspective – '*Look how small that dog is down there*' – was often memorable for young people feeling constrained in the small spaces of families and institutions, holding too many responsibilities. I hoped something would unfold and reveal itself.

## Before…

In fact, the Merrow Downs had housed an Italian prisoner-of-war camp in the 1940s. Remnants of the camp structure remain – the concrete pillars that once supported the watch-towers – and a spectral presence of the prisoners' huts can be seen on Google maps, with all the appearance of a rib-cage that once held its breath.

And before that…

### The forerunners

We allow you to extract flint and chalk, to the extent that it does not impede the commoners' rights to graze and gather fuel.
We allow the gathering of furze, but only as much as can be carried on the back of one man.
We allow you to graze your animals at the density of five sheep, a cow or a bullock per stint.
We are concerned with beautifying the landscape, and the privileges of walking, playing games and recreating.
We allow you to make links and play golf and to park only in designated areas.
We notice the amount of damage caused to the trees and undergrowth in the efforts to find Mrs Christie.

Please let me do my stint. I calculate my entitlement at a quarter of a sheep, and I promise to be careful in any further quests for missing authors.
(Based on extracts from the minutes of Merrow Downs Conservators)

## Protecting and holding places...

I learned recently that a therapist I had been to in my late 20s and early 30s had died some years ago. In the shock and sadness of realising that he had been dead these past four years, I find myself remembering the long drive across London in the early mornings, the traffic jams, the place I stopped on a yellow line to buy dates, the 'building a library' programme that I listened to on the way home. Eventually I find myself thinking about the therapist's waiting room, later still his consulting room. I am keeping at bay the thinking about him, the experience that was him and me. I am letting the place and my journey to and from it protect it.

## Collisions in time: looking for meaning...

What is it that makes the link between inner landscapes of thoughts and feelings and external landscapes of places and the way we behave in them? We have histories. I have proposed a combination – though, depending on the emotional resonances, it could also be a collision – of factors (Izod, 2016: 115):

- the immediate experience of being in this place, now
- a moment in my own history that comes to mind – my 'autobiographic memory'
- my memory comprising sense impressions, their accompanying emotions and behaviours, laid down in my 'procedural memory' (Crittenden, 2005: 259–277).

They give rise to the kind of experiences encountered in déja-vu moments, or in hard-to-grasp, somehow already known experiences that Bollas describes as 'the unthought known' (Bollas,1987: 4), when something is deeply familiar but has not yet surfaced into awareness. In this sense, places have the potential to reveal meanings to us.

> Memories prick the
> mind like sloes readying for
> the first rush of gin...

## Thin places…

I'm attracted to the idea of 'thin places' – places where, according to the Celts, the gap between heaven and earth grows thin and it is easier to encounter the sacred. I transfer this thinking to the secular, to the kind of deeply felt encounter with the self that I have just described: a sense of being in one's element (Izod, 2012: 229), in a place where new meanings become possible. Where are these places – mountains, museums, beds, sheds, therapy rooms?

The anthropologist Ann Armbrecht, in her own journey to explore the boundaries between the self and the fabric of the world, proposes that thin places are 'places where one's nerve endings are bare' (Armbrecht, 2009: 87). It suggests to me the kind of experiences that send a shiver when one is close to awareness or a realisation that comes with inhabiting these in-between spaces, making connections in one's mind.

Healy, curating the exhibition 'Thin Place' (2015: 8), and Armbrecht both reference Virginia Woolf's *The Waves*: 'There are moments when the walls of my mind grow thin, when nothing is unabsorbed' (Woolf, 1931, cited in Armbrecht, 2009: frontispiece). So we are in the terrain of boundaries: the porousness of the boundaries in our minds, the extent to which we can encounter places in an undefended way, absorbing feelings from our environments and letting ourselves be influenced by them. And, at the same time, allowing our imaginations to project themselves into places, to let thoughts and feelings take on physical forms.

The train is held on the bridge at Newport/Casnewydd. Father, to young boy:

> *Take a picture, take a picture of the mud.*
> *What's that place behind it, can you see?*
> *Take a picture, see what comes out?*

I strain forward to see what this man has seen and is asking his son to capture with his camera. It isn't obvious. Mostly there is mud and more mud, a muddy river Usk, making its way into the Bristol Channel. But the idea of what is lying behind what we can see, and the wish for another way to access it, is powerful. Is this a 'thin place' for the father, if not for me? And does he hope, as is not unknown (Sontag, 1976), that the camera can see more than the naked eye; will reveal something more; can be the vehicle that takes him into the place of otherness, of sense-making, myth-making?

## Collision moments: the topoanalytic space...

I am visiting a friend in his new home. It has not been an easy move. As I am lying, up in his attic bedroom, with the rain coming down on the velux windows, the words 'I don't want to be here' repeat over and over in my mind. Where has this come from? Is this my own experience or does it belong to the house and its new resident? Is it one of those collision moments? I root around in my memories. My own childhood bedroom was in an attic space, where I both felt the excitement of being alone and the privacy that it offered, yet a long way from a parent who could hear me if I needed. What was I picking up on?

> Memories as birds
> set up by marauding dogs.
> Wait, don't shoot them down...

It is a long time since I last slept in an attic room. Attics, as Bachelard reminds us in his *Poetics of Space* (1992), offer a place of clarity, the structure a framework for the imagination. Here, in my friend's house, I am in a familiar territory, while also estranged from it. The unconscious rises into my mental awareness – it provides me with a topoanalytic space – a landscape of a remembered past woven into an existing presence. It offers me a locus for the imagination (Izod, 2015).[1]

## Working in the 'here and now'...

Working from a relational systems-psychodynamic background as an organisational consultant makes much use (as does therapeutic

---

1. See also http://culturalstudiesnow.blogspot.co.uk/2011/06/gaston-bachelard-poetics -of-space_23.html (accessed 14 May 2019).

work) of the 'here and now'. 'Now' seems to me to be the containing element of this combination, bounded by and often intensified by time. 'Here', though, appears to offer something more fluid and open to the imagination – what thoughts and feelings are evoked by this room, this street, this neighbourhood? Who can I be here? Yet my experience is that 'here' is the under-developed aspect of 'here and now', even though it frames transference phenomena and is available for exploration as a shifting dynamic: the unconscious transferring of thoughts and feelings from one place and time to another place and time.

Another way of looking at this is through the lens of sensory experience and attachment theory. Places evoke sensory experiences – warmth, cold, security, fear, pleasure, threat – and these experiences accompany us in multiple interactions with our earliest care-givers, being both mediated by and constructed through those interactions. This is the sensory context of development laid down in our procedural memories: automatically evoked repertoires of responses and behaviours, which take their form in our attachment patterning. So, transference is something that is not just projected and identified with but evoked and provoked by lived experience – an experience that is itself drenched with place and our associations with it.

## Walking and talking…

I am preparing for a walk and talk that I will be giving as part of the Tavistock Institute Festival,[2] and am visiting Tavistock Square Gardens in Bloomsbury with an Australian colleague. I've called the event 'Here is Where I Am', in response to Margaret Tait's 1964 film *Where I Am is Here*. By it, I am inferring that 'here' is a place in which I have a presence; without my own presence, it would be 'there', so that place evokes a dynamic sense of self, and self and place become interwoven (Izod, 2016: 118). On this sunny August morning, the gardens are a place of recreation: students are picnicking; a group of people are practising t'ai chi; memorials are bedecked with flowers and ribbons; a benign warmth permeates.

---

2. http://festival.tavinstitute.org/event/here-is-where-i-am/ (accessed 13 May 2019).

We are trying to find the original location of the Tavistock Institute of Medical Psychology, which evolved into both the present-day Tavistock and Portman NHS Foundation Trust and the Tavistock Institute of Human Relations. It looks as if it no longer exists as a separate building with its own front door. In the search for this place, we become curious and bold. We engage with receptionists of other buildings and get their help. People are interested. We can assume the mantle of tourists, even though that belies the significance of the task we are doing.

## Identity...

Working on one's identity is, I think, a constantly revisable research activity about places that are important or have been significant and who and what I have been able to be and can be in those places. Much of my consulting and coaching work with groups and individuals concerns identity: either the identity that I bring to or that is evoked in taking up a role, or the identity that an organisation conveys through its brand and reputation. In this kind of identity work, I make use of social theories of development (Bowlby, 1969; Fairbairn, 1952), with their emphasis on attachment and the drive for connection, together with their implications for individual and group behaviour.

'Who am I now?' and 'Where am I now?' are orientating questions (Izod, 2015: 11–25) that prove helpful in disorientating places such as group life, where loss of a sense of self and the threat to one's identity (Turquet, 1975) are common experiences. So questions to support and sustain identities in such situations include:

- Do I **recognise** myself in this place – does it (as with Gollan Head) mirror back to me something recognisable about who I am?

- How does this place evoke other and different identities? Who can I be here? Which of my identities are capable of being mobilised, or **revealed** here? (I think of myself in holiday mode, more risk-taking, more fun-loving, perhaps).

- And how does this place impact on and help me **regulate** my feelings? Does it offer something secure or more threatening?

I think of places as 'transitional spaces', in Winnicott's language (Winnicott, 1969: 86–94), there to allow for experimentation, the trying out of possibilities.

## Knowing one's place…

I am talking about place with a group of social scientists via a webcam group. We come from Europe, the Caribbean, Africa, the US, the UK, yet the space we are meeting in is virtual, in the mind, contained by a history of meeting at a certain time, over time. An idea emerges about 'knowing one's place', and in this context our conversation moves into the dynamics of power, oppression, one's personal place in the social stratification of relations, a country's political position in the global order. This is not only about knowing but about being 'put in one's place', as if this can only ever be a singular entity. The rights to be nomadic or itinerant are imperilled as border controls tighten, as walls in the mind become walls in reality.

## Being a nomad…

Yet therapeutic work, or work on role, relies on the nomadic capacity of the mind to wander across landscapes, to stimulate and support a curiosity that may have been shut down for personal, cultural or political reasons.

Being a nomad implies a lightness of foot, carrying just the necessities for survival and one's journeying across changing terrains. Working on ideas about familiarisation and estrangement in Seamus Heaney's poems, Cowper (2009: 168) explores his response to the question: 'How does the self continue, when the people and places that once helped define it are gone?' My immediate answer to this is that we hoard; we hoard those things that come to represent the lost place, the lost person; we hoard memorabilia.

> This is my baggage.
> I could leave it here, but will
> I find it again?

This is, of course, my non-nomad self, imagining loss of place, rather than the carrying and absorbing of place within one's self. I'm far from being displaced, though familiar with what it is when one's mind wanders too far from home. I am familiar too with the shedding of aspects of the self in the seeking of different places in the mind from which to set out; in the disentangling of the mind from the emotions that keep it to fixed positions (Benjamin, 1998).

## Staying...

> Memories, short-lived
> as a politician's. Stay
> a-while, here are roots.

I have been living in the same house for 30 years (another way of knowing my place/knowing this place) and know this to be a rare security afforded by place. My garden is slowly taking on the characteristics of the nearby downland, with a growing profusion of ox-eye daisies, pyramid orchids, bird's eye trefoils and wild marjoram. At the end of this suburban garden is a small triangle of land that we have left to grow wild, and it is largely untouched. Dead wood lies where it falls. Over time, the once functional shed has completely covered itself with ivy, which hangs in dusty sheets through the gaps in the roof. The floor has rotted and been undermined by foxes, perhaps rats. Wasps' nests attach to window frames. Inside is the detritus of old bicycles and broken chairs. It is the reality of a place left to itself, and sometimes I think that we should pull it down, but I leave it there, existing in the periphery of my experience. I am not sure what it symbolises and can think of it as a place of natural decay and re-generation, which allows me a slow-burning curiosity. I am, though, more inclined to view it as an attempt at a permanence, which is nonetheless in a constant state of fragility and flux, and which another person at another time, might come and tidy away (for which substitute re-develop, re-possess, devastate, bomb).

## Coincidences...

WG Sebald, a great itinerant, might have had some queries about the coincidence/collision of memory and of experience that I've mentioned earlier. In his conversation with Tim Parkes (2000), he suggests that coincidences are punctuations in life, cutting across or through experience to tell us this has happened before, or this has happened to someone else before. They are a reminder that we are not unique. Talking with a friend, I heard how her son, then aged about six, had met a child he knew at the top of Snowdon and had been unsurprised. There was someone he knew, and she was at the top of Snowdon. Only once we get older do the mathematics of coincidence, the 'unlikelihoods' of chance, start to intervene in our willingness to accept that these random acts do happen.

## Return...

Returning to St Deiniol's[3] library one April, I had begun a piece of writing on the nature of 'return' when, looking out of the window, I saw and heard my first sightings of the swifts. It isn't unusual for me to be delighted by their arrival; they happen upon me more than I find myself looking out for them. And I have been thinking about writing about the nature of return for while. Now, they have conjoined in a way that I give meaning to; I allow myself to symbolise the swifts as agents of a capacity to return. It excites, delights, interrupts, and enables me to be here, in this present.

## Time zones...

I have several times been, and returned to, St Deiniol's and these visits are punctuated by the intervenings of life in six-monthly chunks. It sets me off to think about change. Are these the same lampshades, is this the same shade of green on the walls? Where are the comfy chairs in the dining room? Progress brings its changes, and when I am here I am in touch with the wish for things to remain constant, for there to have been very little human touch to the surroundings that I have and still enjoy so much. And then I have my touchstone for what is changing, what I can see that has come about in its stead, and I can appreciate it not necessarily as a replacement or as filling an absence but as something newly present.

---

3. Now re-named Gladstone's library, Flintshire.

Standing in the queue for supper one night, I spoke with a young woman here to research for her thesis. She didn't know whether the green was the same this year as last; she was encountering it for the first time. My 'new' was her 'already here', and unless she was prompted in some way to spend much of her time thinking about what was here before she encountered it – at the level of colour, taste, smell, human experience – then her present is a present not encountered at a level of the past. We stood in a queue in different time zones.

## Streams of consciousness…

My mother, who cannot remember what she did a moment ago, asks me repeatedly if I remember when her road was a dirt road with a stream running down it. Forty years ago there were streams criss-crossing the village and they are now underground, largely built over. I, who (presently) do remember what I did a moment ago, have no recollection of this, although at some level it rings a bell. I speculate that she made some kind of connection with the streams; that she, a newcomer, moving out to this semi-rural village, had invested in them, and that I, living there only for a few years when my mind and direction in life were centred elsewhere, had not. The move to this village was imbued with hope, a new beginning and, in particular for my mother, a move away from her family roots where she had been born and lived her early married life. The streams have come back to her now as a powerful image at a time when her present ability to give meaning to her surroundings is impaired. A meaning of place is working away in her.

## What if I didn't know? …

Often when I am talking with people about what a place means to them, I meet with the response, 'If I didn't know about the history of this place, then I wouldn't feel what I do about it. I only get this feeling because I've read on the interpretation board that this is where there used to be a gunpowder manufactory, or here is where there was an atrocity.' Ah, but you do know about it, I say, or you know that sometime in the life of this place, something happened. So, there is a different question to ask: 'Knowing what I know happened then, what do I know or feel now? How far back in history does a moment affect the now: a minute, a decade, a millennium?'

## Walking and talking revisited…

Returning to Tavistock Square Gardens in October, it is a dark and wet day, wind gathers the leaves along the paths and fetches them up against the plinths of the statues with their jam jars of dying blooms. Overhead the leaves are vivid in reds and purples. I am with a group of people, perhaps a dozen of us, exploring the sense of place given over by this London square. It is the event that I had been preparing for back in August. Apart from us and the occasional other person passing briskly through, the square is empty. No students idling on the grass, no t'ai chi, no leisurely lunches. It is not really a place to linger, though we do, and the group drifts into solitary and silent exploration.

One participant is taken aback by the collision of events that happened here, or which have been memorialised here: how does one London square attract wartime bombing, suicide, terrorism, violence and conscientious objection to taking up arms? The summery sense of place that gave rise to my more playful and inquisitive self has been replaced by an autumnal self that accords more weight to the atrocities of life than to their reparation and reconciliation. The square has become more urban, traffic noise permeates, someone sees a rat running across a path. The tree planted in memory of Hiroshima, ribbons tied to its branches in the summer, now has a dishevelled look to it. How do you decorate such a tree? What do you choose to put on it? It is a reminder that encounters with places are fleeting, exist in the moment that I am present, become both what I bring to it and it brings forth from me.

## Meaning-making…

Lauren Elkin, exploring this same square in London on the trail of Virginia Woolf, writes (after Yi-Fu Tuan, 1977: 6) that places are spaces that we imbue with meaning (Elkin, 2016: 21). As we walk and talk, we cross boundaries – the boundaries of the gardens, with their iron railings that enclose them, and the boundaries of the square, with its buildings and roads on all four sides. It is an example of an open system (Miller & Rice, 1967), its boundaries existing in the reality of the streets and railings and in the mind and where we will let the mind go. Inside, the gardens have become associated with peace and reconciliation; outside in the square is the reminder of the terrorist suicide bombings of July 2005. Is this a coincidence? The place offers ambiguity, divergence. Can a collective meaning-making happen here?

## On the move...

I meet a colleague for lunch. I talk with him about what I am thinking about place, our attachment to places, how we might seek out new and unfamiliar places to enrich our experiences and inevitably have to lose old and familiar places that may also have enriched our lives. His office is about to move. They are down-sizing, with Brexit pushing at their international doors and pushing the place/identity/belonging questions: where is the UK? What can our company be here? Who can we be here?

Patterns of work will change. Less space means hot-desking and working from home; space and who has access to which spaces become contested in talk about who is going where and whether hot-desks can be personalised, whether photos, plants and papers can be left out overnight and whether the nomad self will have to shed its belongings.

This is an example of the use of place as an intervention into a system, with all its possibilities for change. Working as a consultant to effect change is an action-orientated process, in which place is an element that can be brought into experimental 'play'. It brings to mind an organisational intervention to move a 'forgotten' office at the far end of a long government corridor into a more central position, both in the corridor and in people's minds.

The issue of belonging, of finding one's place within an organisation, evokes the dynamics of identity that I spoke of earlier. While my colleague's organisation might not have chosen to move, it is moving; its landscape is already shifting and, with it, the internal worlds of its staff are encountering new terrains of possibility and constraint.

## Haunting…

To speak a bit about absence – a lack, something expected in a place that is not there and that might be encountered as a haunting.

I am thinking of haunting as something that remains persistently at the edges of memory, that sits uncomfortably on the edges of consciousness. Returning to one's old haunts is often an unsettling experience, a wish to regain something that has been lost or to re-confirm or validate a memory that would otherwise be doubtful. Returning to Cowper's chapter (2009), she explores the space where memory and experience interweave, how memory can become dislocated from experience and experience from time.

Seamus Heaney writes in 'Midnight Anvil' (2006: 22–23):

If I wasn't there
When Barney Devlin hammered
The midnight anvil
I can still hear it.

This is the kind of 'porousness' of mind and attunement with one's environment that can play with time and place and allow for the kind of shifts away from the 'here and now' that are not so much a flight from the present as an opening out in one's imagination. One of my fellow walkers in Tavistock Square Gardens wrote afterwards how walking and talking with other participants, noticing what they had expected from the place but was noticeably absent, had set up a shared curiosity, where the potential for work, for new associations (with people and in the mind) were emerging from the present. The emotional work to relate to this place, existing in a past and a present, had enabled a projective space to emerge in which one's own relatedness to 'Tavistock' could be engaged with in a way that also suggested a future. Did she hear 'the midnight anvil' and when might it have been ringing in her memory and in her imagination?

## Recognition revisited…

### Gollan Head: former home to RAF radar station, Outer Hebrides

*I recognise this place, its air saturated*
*With the echo-waves of a spent force ten.*
*Horizontal spume strays into squat pebble-dash*
                    *recedes behind barred windows*
            *their panes blind with the permanence of plastic.*

*No trusting to direction out here,*
*No radio to detect the near and far,*
*Nor pulse to testify, to reassure.*

*The gate fastens, its padlock clinging*
*emptily to a fallen cliff.*
*A fissure, a fulmar's chink,*
*still hold the weight of abandon.*

*In bare streets, new lives thread.*
*Dogs and tricycles weave haphazard.*

*Unregiment*

## Not an ending…

Revisiting Gollan Head was to encounter a difference where the agitation of my first visit had lessened. At some level I had wanted to re-create that earlier experience, which had stayed with me, perhaps even haunted me, over several years. There was a sense of loss at knowing that my experience belonged to just that particular collision of time and place. At some level, I wished I had let the memory be, let it reside in the mind with the mutual recognition it offered. It was, after all, familiar.

## Acknowledgements

With thanks for the contributions of colleagues and participants at 'Here is Where I am' Tavistock Festival, October 2017, and members of the AK Rice (Chicago) virtual reading groups. Also for conversations with colleagues and friends whose stories have made their way into this work.

With thanks to Jill Munro and Sarah Miles, editors of *Best of British* (Paper Swans Press, 2017), where 'Gollan Head: former home to RAF radar station, Outer Hebrides' was first published.

## References

Armbrecht A (2009). *Thin Places: a pilgrimage home*. New York, NY: Columbia University Press.

Bachelard G (1992). *Poetics of Space*. Boston, MA: Beacon Press.

Benjamin J (1998). *Shadow of the Other: intersubjectivity and gender in psychoanalysis*. New York, NY: Routledge.

Bollas C (1987). *The Shadow of the Object: psychoanalysis of the unthought known*. New York, NY: Columbia University Press.

Bowlby J (1969). *Attachment and Loss, Volume 1: attachment*. London: Hogarth Press.

Cowper J (2009). 'The places I go back to': familiarisation and estrangement in Seamus Heaney's later poetry. In: Brewster S, Parker M (eds). *Irish Literature Since 1990*. Manchester: Manchester University Press (pp160–176).

Crittenden PM (2005). Internal representational models of attachment relationships. *Infant Mental Health Journal 11*(3): 259–277.

Elkin L (2016). *Flâneuse: women walk the city in Paris, New York, Tokyo, Venice and London*. London: Random House.

Fairbairn W (1952). *Psychoanalytic Studies of the Personality*. London: Tavistock Publications.

Healy C (2015). *Thin Place*. Carmarthen: Oriel Myrddin Gallery/Arts Council Wales.

Heaney S (2006). *District and Circle*. London: Faber & Faber.

Izod K (2017). Gollan Head: former home to RAF radar station, Outer Hebrides. In: Miles S, Munro J (eds). *Best of British*. UK: Paper Swans Press (p36).

Izod K (2016). Representation, place and equivalent realities: an exploration of relational perspectives on representation and meaning. *Organisational and Social Dynamics 16*(1): 100–128.

Izod K (2015). *A View from the Attic*. [Blog.] Karnacology. https://karnacology.com/ art-and-therapy/a-view-from-the-attic-karen-izod-on-place-and-memory/ (accessed 5 December 2017).

Izod K (2012). Elemental. *Attachment: New Directions in Psychotherapy and Relational Psychoanalysis 6*(3): 228–231.

Merrow Downs Conservators. *Minute Book*. Woking: Surrey History Centre. www. exploringsurreyspast.org.uk/collections/getrecord/SHCOL_BR_PART3_6_11_2_2 (accessed 20 April 2018).

Miller EJ, Rice AK (1967). *Systems of Organization: task and sentient systems and their boundary controls*. London: Tavistock Publications.

Parkes T (2000). The Hunter. *New York Review of Books*; 15 June. Reprinted in: Schwartz LS (ed) (2007). *The Emergence of Memory: conversations with WG Sebald*. New York, NY: Seven Stories Press (pp23–36).

Sontag S (1976). Introduction. In: Huljar P. *Portraits in Life and Death*. Boston, MA: Da Capo Press.

Tuan Y-F (1977). *Space and Place: the perspectives of experience*. Minneapolis, MN: University of Minnesota Press (p6).

Turquet P (1975). Threats to identity in the large group. In: Kreeger L (ed). *The Large Group: dynamics and therapy*. London: Constable (pp87–114).

Winnicott DW (1969). The use of an object and relating through identifications. In: Winnicott DW (1971). *Playing and Reality*. London: Tavistock Publications (pp86–94).

Woolf V (1931). *The Waves*. London: Hogarth Press.

# 9 | 'Not in the air and not on earth': on negotiating the states in between

## Valentina Krajnović

Have you ever been going along, living your life, living in your reality, and then something happens that rips your world right in two? You see something or hear something, and suddenly everything you are, everything you are doing, shatters into thousand shards of sharp, bitter realisations. (Tiernan, 2011: 1)

Almost exactly half of my life ago, in 1992, I got on a plane in Belgrade and flew to London. I needed some time out of my own country, then called Yugoslavia, to attempt to make sense of what was happening there at the time.

I came to the UK as I hoped to train in group analysis. I wanted to understand groups better, especially larger ones, and my own country in particular. I wanted to make more sense of how they could grow and survive, particularly when communication within did not seem possible. I wondered how the existing anxieties and fears could be managed, both acknowledged and thought about: the fears of fragmentation, alienation, abandonment and the lack of belonging, the threat of loss, of being excommunicated, put in exile.

It took me some time to realise this, but I was also facing my own life transition. I was looking for home, as the country and the city I was inhabiting had in some way stopped feeling like one, at least at the time. I craved the possibility of finding a new point of view, a different angle on life, people and politics.

I had many questions:

- What is home? A place where we can be ourselves? A place where we feel safe and people around us are safe? Both, I imagine, and many other things…
- How does one decide whether to make a nest somewhere new or not?
- How does one embrace the process of transition from one city to another, from one country to another, from one socio-political system and culture to another, from one physical and geographical climate to another?

I believed that, in the interconnection between myself and my newly acquired surroundings, something different would emerge. And I wondered, would I become more or less of myself in this particular place I had come to inhabit?

## The place

The way I went about mapping my answers to all these questions was possibly somewhat unorthodox. I put my resources into getting to know London, the city, first, I guess as a representation of the UK. I wanted to find some familiarity, which seemed more easily done focusing on the geographical environment. I also thought that finding out about the city might be one of the ways to get to know its people.

In a therapeutic encounter, I would strive to create a setting that was safe enough to enable growth and development. I set out to do something similar for myself in the world outside, finding Winnicott's idea of the environmental mother very helpful at this time (Winnicott, 1971). I also decided to subscribe to a known therapeutic and life-actualising principle and go into something new as open as I could be. I wanted to allow myself a free-floating engagement (Foulkes, 1964) with the reality, before any contemplation was to happen.

What helped me follow this maxim was that my mind actually felt like a tabula rasa. I did not know what my journey into the unknown might entail. Hence, I was like a clean slate, waiting to be scribbled on by what occurred in between myself and the world around me.

And that was when my walks became invaluable. They helped me begin to embrace this particular in-between state of mind and being, the interplay between my inner and the outer world. I was in search of home, both symbolic and a real one. Meanwhile, potential homelessness was lurking in the corners of my existence and the underground of this new city. Nevertheless, there was one part of my experience that was less puzzling: it actually seemed easier to not belong in a foreign country than to feel that I did not belong in what I considered to be my own country.

A very important person in my life, my brother, used to say: 'God help us live during interesting times.' As far as I remember, there was no suggestion that these 'interesting times' would necessarily be easy ones. If anything, I assumed that they needed to be at least reasonably challenging. I kept this in mind.

## Drifting

### On familiarity, the lack of it and the state in between

I set out to explore and get to know London by walking, by the *dérive*:

> … that ambient drifting through the urban environment
> that was to later be defined… as a predominant technique of
> psychogeography; this was in contrast to the technique of a
> flâneur, described as just 'a transient passage through various
> ambiances'. (Coverley, 2018: 96)

Therefore, over the following months, I would fleetingly look at the map of London and vanish into the city. Invariably, I would discover myself somewhere new and unfamiliar.

I drifted through the new spaces, soaking in the smells, the forms, the shapes and the sounds of the city. I remember the strange but often pleasant type of holding that drifting provided me with at the time.

### The Thames

What was particularly striking in my free-floating journeys was that I would so often end up near the Thames. I would cross it on foot, over one of the bridges, and stop in the middle to breathe, look and immerse myself in the world around me. This became a way to feel rooted and at home in my surroundings. For a moment at least, I would feel free, not trapped at a crossroad between two spaces, two sides, and I would become aware of the changes both in myself and in the world around me.

There are very similarly positioned bridges over the river Sava in the centre of Belgrade, from Old Town to New Belgrade. These bridges were where I spent many crucial moments during my life, drifting into the surrounding spaces and re-finding myself in the process. It was also where I first dared acknowledge, to myself and a friend of mine, the stifling concern and confusion I had about the rumours: my country was said to be on the brink of a civil war that could destroy and devour any possibility of a peaceful negotiation and eventual acceptance of the differences within it.

I recall having nightmares about the two parts of Belgrade, divided by the river, splitting apart and becoming so completely cut off that the connection could never be made again. I would wake up with a sense of nameless dread (Bion, 1962), wondering about the fantasised schism and what might happen if it ever came to fruition.

It all seemed a premonition of the events to come, although it was not Belgrade that split apart but my whole country, which was crushed into fragments some years later.

## The Barbican

Another place I felt I could easily wander into following my arrival was the Barbican complex.[1]

This is a distinctive urban oasis in the centre of London, on the north-east side of the river. In one way, I loved its shape and its nestling feel, its height and sharp edges. But I also repeatedly felt an uncanny sense within me whenever I entered the complex:

---

1. The Barbican complex was built during the 1960s and the 1980s in the City of London, on a site devastated by bombing in World War II. It is a prominent example of British brutalist architecture and comprises the residential Barbican Estate, the Barbican Arts Centre, the Museum of London, the Guildhall School of Music and Drama and the Barbican Public Library. Since 2006, it has hosted an annual Battle of Ideas festival 'to discuss the big issues of our time' (www.battleofideas.org.uk).

> The uncanny involves feelings of uncertainty, in particular regarding the reality of who one is and what is being experienced. Suddenly one's sense of oneself... seems strangely questionable... But uncanny is not simply an experience of strangeness and alienation. More specifically, it is a peculiar commingling of the familiar and unfamiliar. (Royle, 2003: 1)

This tall, dark structure seemed both safe and mysteriously unsafe: familiar, as though I had always known it, and very fresh and unfamiliar, however many times I visited. It often felt empty, although people would be present, so it seemed both full and hollow.

The sounds reverberated peculiarly and beautifully there. They reminded me of the homely sounds of my childhood in a capital city, within a sepia-hued sturdiness. The concrete edifice felt warm and vibrant in its solidity. However, it also had a lonely and alienating echo, unhomely and rigid. In her writings on abjection, philosopher, psychoanalyst and literary critic Julia Kristeva (Kristeva, 1991) talked about the experience of strangeness and depersonalisation as integral in creating contemporary subjectivity. I found her thinking helpful in my attempt to embrace this cosmopolitan city.

At the time, I often wondered if there was a connection between what a particular city or community needed and how and if this was related to the process of designing buildings in general. I contemplated the kind of city that would support the evolution of communication among its different communities and groups of people. What would facilitate the inclusion of everyone in a more democratic way, what would nurture a sense of togetherness, of fellowship, which I felt my own city and country lacked, certainly at that moment in time?

Nevertheless, walking through the Barbican, I could still lose myself in the timeless sea of the quiet. And I also stayed on tiptoe, prepared to act if this feeling changed into something else, something unforthcoming or threatening. This had been a surreal, dreamlike experience, somewhere in between my subjective imagination and what could be perceived as an objective reality.

Was this a symbolic parallel to how I actually felt in London as a whole – in between worlds? Was I roaming through it like 'a temple in clouds, not in the air and not on earth'[2] – both in 1992 and later on, in 1999, as my own country was literally collapsing?

I believe the Barbican complex helped me stay in touch with my own in-between state of being. I was existing within and between at least two worlds and I needed time to link them peacefully. These worlds were to me, above all, uncertain. Well, I am the daughter of the Balkans, where uncertainty has been the way of life: where bridges have been built and broken or blown up; where people have lived together and then grown or been split apart, as though there was no history of their previous existence; where history could be rewritten, maybe too easily, considering the amount of effort put into making it initially.

## The people

### On looking, being seen and the space in between

When I think about it now, I possibly focused on getting to know the city first because I was wary of getting to know its citizens. As it happened, some of my initial experiences with people were not particularly easy or straightforward.

I remember being at a gathering with a friend and being asked by a young woman if people in Yugoslavia had phones and washing machines. I did not know how to respond; rapid anger and sadness both seemed to be clouding my mind. I was puzzled by my quick reactions.

I felt I had been put in the position of a victim of my Balkan culture. I very much disliked being considered a poor daughter of this presumably underdeveloped part of the world: at the crossroads between East and West, North and South, where people did not seem to learn and grow. I was pained by the sense of being taken for a mere follower of Communism rather than a person in my own right. I had at times been choked by the strength of the

---

2. 'Čardak ni na Nebu ni na Zemlji' is the title of a Serbian folk tale that literally translates as 'The Castle/Temple not in the Air and not on Earth' (my own translation). It can also be interpreted as 'The Temple in the Clouds'.

prejudices and the feelings they provoked in me. I read later that: 'Various Balkan nations symbolically define themselves as being at a gate, on a bridge, or at a crossroads between different worlds' (Goldsworthy, 1998: 18), between East and West.

> While an 'enlightened, democratic West' defines itself in terms of contrast to a 'despotic East', the 'industrious', rational culture of the North claims a position of superiority over the 'undisciplined', passionate cultures of southern Europe, establishing a kind of European hierarchy in which the north-west represents the highest and the south-east the lowest symbolic value. (Goldsworthy, 1998: 20)

I was not sure if I wanted to fit into the culture that often seemed so ill-informed and dismissive of my own heritage. I joined the training at the Institute of Group Analysis (IGA) because I wished to engage once again in mutual connection with others. I wished to see the others and to be mirrored back in return – to be seen for who I was or was becoming.

## Mirroring

I became more curious about the process of mirroring among people. I looked at it as a way of negotiating the space in between, as a primal way of communicating and changing, a connection that would hopefully bridge the gap between people (Jaćimović, 1998).

Mirror reactions characteristically occur when a number of people meet and interact. A person sees herself – often a repressed part of herself – reflected in the actions of other group members. She sees them reacting in the way she does herself, or unlike her own behaviour. She also gets to know herself – and this is a fundamental process in ego development – by the effect she has upon others and the picture they form of her (Foulkes, 1964: 110).

However, I knew that people could become alienated from one another if there was a continual mismatch in their communication. Jeff Roberts (1993), a group analyst, compares the analytic group to a hall of mirrors. The effect of finding oneself in such a hall of mirrors could, in his opinion, be experienced as beneficial to the individual and group, contributing to the development of both, or as intensely persecuting: 'Seeing one's self reflected through the group process can lead to concern, transformation and growth, but it can also precipitate rage, panic, denial and flight' (Roberts, 1993: 95).

I remember attending an event on 'Endings in Psychotherapy' at the IGA in 1993, organised by the Jungian and group analyst Louis Zinkin. During a particular discussion in my small group, I was asked by one of the participants, a former priest, what I would do if somebody killed my brother. He wanted to know if I could then also kill, as a Serbian at war. I remember looking into the eyes of the man asking me the question and, luckily, seeing his own fury with something unnamed. Nevertheless, I was speechless. I did not find a way of answering him. I was so relieved when the group leader involved the group as a whole in contemplating our own shadows and how easy it would be to choose to see something only in another. Hence, what initially seemed invasive and harmful turned into a beautiful process of mutual reflective mirroring within the group. I experienced a full connection with the others and felt I could see them differently. I also felt seen and protected as the whole person I am, including my cultural heritage. And that happened at a particularly provocative time in history, when it seemed to me that Serbia was being reported by the media in the UK and some parts of Europe as the worst, the cruellest side in the Yugoslavian civil war.

It was only later that I read Zinkin's musings on the mirroring process that could somehow go 'horribly wrong, like the distorting mirror in a fun fair' (Zinkin, 1983: 114). He called it malignant mirroring and warned of its destructive nature. I realised how deeply he understood and embraced its dangers. Yet he also managed, in my experience, to facilitate a peaceful transformation of toxicity into communication and connection, however imperfect.

And thinking about the here and now in 2018, it still seems appropriate to reflect on and write about the importance of mirroring and the dangers of malignant mirroring on both small and wider scales. At this moment in the history of Europe and the world, boundaries, borders and connections continue to be attacked and challenged on a daily basis.

This sense of in between in the present time closely mirrors for me both the time when I moved to the UK in 1992 and the later moments when my own country of birth was inevitably disintegrating, as we were on the threshold of the 21st century.

I pondered how to explain what really happened in the civil war in Yugoslavia. I wondered if my own understanding was sufficient. I realised that I could only offer my own reflections on this part of history, coloured by the things I knew about and the ones I didn't, at least not at the time. I also hoped that, in a small way, this could illuminate what might be happening in the world at this point, with its further wars, the consequent destruction, loss of lives and widespread fragmentation.

## Remembering

### On memory, desire and the existence in between

After my move to the UK and through the later years of the war raging in my country of origin, I was acutely aware of the coexistence of life and death. Memory and the reworking of historical reality seemed of paramount importance, in order to get close enough to the truth of the present and build a bridge towards a possible future.

I remembered a family story from World War Two that I first heard from my cousin when I was in my teens. I still see it vividly. My father's mother, his four siblings and he himself were among many Serbian families crossing the river Drina, from Bosnia where their home had been, to Serbia, fleeing from the Germans and the Croatian Ustashe. His father was in the resistance, fighting the enemy back in Bosnia and covering their escape. A lot of the families had several children, all needing to be taken care of, with very little water and food available. Unable to manage them all, some of the devastated mothers were throwing their own crying babies into the river, so that they could protect the remaining children and also keep them quiet enough to escape.

I can still recall my father's pained eyes when retelling the story and my mother's shock on hearing it for the first time some years later, after the civil war had already started. My mother was a few years younger than my father; she was born and raised in Belgrade by her Ukrainian parents and had experienced the war differently. As the eldest son, my father was already carrying some responsibility for his family. He was frightened by the possibility of his youngest brother being thrown into the river. He shared the load of carrying him, despite being only 11 years old at the time, so his brother could stay safe. He had been grateful that all of his siblings survived.

I mulled over this and some other memories during my blurred walks through the woods on Hampstead Heath. At times I would rest on the banks of the lake there, often not fully aware of the beauty and aliveness of the nature around me but feeling preoccupied and frozen by the cruelty of the wars. While remembering what I knew of my country's history during the 20th century as a whole, I also attempted to distinguish the imprints of my core family and their ancestors. I needed to remember the past, as anything new could only be created upon its imprint. I felt that, if I forgot this, I could lose something very important – an interwoven part of my own, my family's and my country's histories.

I wanted to give a structure to these messy, blurred experiences – experiences of the war itself, of friends becoming enemies. I wanted to understand the pain of separation and alienation from the other – the expansion of the space in between. I also wanted to understand the fear of closeness, where the space in between might shrink into an unhealthy merger.

The process of drifting through the mouldy vastness of the woodland allowed me to breathe and bear the experience of loss and sorrow. In my heart, I carried the devastating events that were happening – the horrors done to my people as well as the ones done by them; both were achingly difficult to digest. Was I only an observer in all of this, or a participant, however distant? My walks supported me in getting hold of the space between different realities and stories, including my own, in order to counteract my sense of fear, anxiety and displacement.

Nigerian writer Chimamanda Ngozi Adichie, writing about the dangers of focusing on a single story in the context of the civil war in her own country, warns:

> If we hear only a single story about another person or country, we risk a critical misunderstanding… When we reject the single story, when we realise that there is never a single story about any place, we regain a kind of paradise. (Adichie, 2009)

Her novel, *Half of a Yellow Sun* (Adichie, 2006) seems a painfully vibrant and memorable articulation of this belief.

## Losing country and home

In the year 2000, in the horrors and trauma of the civil war, Yugoslavia disappeared from the map of Europe and the world, after 83 years of existence. Slovenia, Macedonia, Bosnia, Croatia, Serbia and Montenegro grew out of the ashes. Belgrade, the former capital of Yugoslavia, became the capital of Serbia, and my birth nationality consequently changed.

Did I feel that I had lost my birth home with the collapse of Yugoslavia after the civil war? In some ways, yes, as I considered myself to be a Yugoslavian. My family held a mixture of heritages, hence I have always felt at home in a mixed environment. Yugoslavia falling apart into more divided but less diverse groupings meant that I had, in a way, lost my country. This loss seemed unfathomable and confusing and I felt naive that I had not predicted it, that I had not seen what, I thought, must have been there to be seen.

During this process of formal fragmentation, which was further accelerated by the NATO bombing of Yugoslavia in 1999, I was writing my clinical paper, the final step towards qualifying as a group analyst. And I was in between countries again, and the world happened to be in between two centuries.

The reality felt so uncertain then. I had been inhaling the uncanny, deep inside of me and that was frightening. However, it was also strangely engaging, provoking my own persistence in looking for the meaning of the experience. And I continued drifting, while searching for and 'slouching towards' (Yeats, 2000) a possible understanding.

I walked, this time with my Walkman, given to me by my brother and named by him a 'Walkwoman'. I let myself get lost in the rhythm of music, in raging and also in soothing tones, again less aware of my surroundings at the time.

I endlessly listened to Mozart's Requiem and my brother's musical pieces, especially to 'La Flamme de l'Orange', 'What is going on?' and 'Mirska Pjenija' (Jaćimović, 1987, 1990, 1993). The music kept eerily capturing my experience with its mirroring sounds and perfectly chosen words. I was attempting to digest the loss, anger, sadness and pain of the reality. I was not sure what had felt worse: not going back to Belgrade to support my family and friends through the bombing, as they pleaded with me not to, or being physically and geographically on the side that was making them suffer so much fear and uncertainty. I felt it was my responsibility to bear the reality and not waver, not give up, not stop thinking, and possibly continue to write about it all, immortalise it somehow.

I longed for the moment when this nightmare would be over and hoped that another reparative reality would approach soon, while I intuitively knew it was not going to be soon enough. It felt so difficult to see the events unfolding and keep an open mind – sometimes almost impossible. I felt unable to help, but I did not lose hope, at least not consciously, however hopeless the reality felt at times. I guess my hopelessness was carried and held in my unconscious through that period, while I held my families in my heart, both the one in Serbia and the one I had in the UK.

I eventually went back to the bridges on the Thames, which I somehow saw as the heart of London – the intersection between the man-made and the natural world. I wondered about my belonging, about my home in Belgrade and my home in London. Was I betraying my mother-tongue city for the foreign-tongue one that had become my home as well? I was distraught that I chose to drift in London and not in Belgrade.

I re-visited the Barbican, looking for peace and solidity. But I found myself, again and again, noticing the pain and the darker side of almost everything I looked at. It seemed as though my surroundings were painted using a sfumato technique, where tones and colours shaded gradually into one another, creating softened outlines or hazy forms. The vagueness and mist I was noticing in my wanderings were there, both in the places I knew and the ones I did not.

'The city is uncanny when it reveals itself in new and unexpected light; when its streets, buildings, and people suddenly appear strange, out of place, and not quite right' (Huskinson, 2016: i). Did I feel that London was a particularly uncanny urban place at the time?

Was I wanting to find this city more ghostly, due to my own inner turmoil, while at the same time I felt at home there, regardless? This must have been so, in some way, however unaware of it I was to start with. I believe I desired both safety and the lustre of freedom, but I also needed the history and complexity of dark shadows, in order for both London and me to feel more authentic and real.

And there it was again, the crossroads: the point when the particular place with its history (the outer world) became so intrinsically connected to its people (and their inner world); when all the moments in the evolution of the place and all the moments in the life of its inhabitants met; the opening towards the uncertainty and hope for there being a future, an eternal wish to develop something new that would embrace the disturbance of the old and allow the continuity of being.

## Writing

### Roaming through the mind

After Yugoslavia disappeared, my walks gradually gave way to writing. I continued drifting but now it was through my own inner galaxy, searching for words that could represent it adequately. I kept the thoughts of psychoanalyst and writer Thomas Ogden in my mind: 'Language is not simply a package in which communications are wrapped, but the medium in which experience is brought to life in the process of being spoken or written' (Ogden 1999: 201).

The process of finding and re-finding words for my own experiences of the inner and the outer reality felt both amazing and torturous at times. It was rich and painful, enlightening and enlivening, but it was also completely mystifying in its re-shaping of the phenomena I was attempting to observe and understand.

I kept writing while roaming through what I could read and draw in from my friends and family. I followed all the streams of consciousness, pre-consciousness and unconsciousness I could find. I had an urge to capture the sense of the experience so it did not get lost. I felt I needed to remember it in order to be able to transfer and translate it to the next generations – to my own children, too, as and when that became appropriate.

My qualifying paper in its final form focused on creation, destruction and recreation (Jaćimović, 1999). I tried to explore how the interplay between creative and destructive forces within a small group – if taken under the auspices of dialogue – could facilitate the processes of transformation and integration of the group and the personal development of its individual participants. I struggled, though, to find the appropriate ways of applying my developing understanding, as imperfect as it was, on a bigger scale.

It was some months later that I stumbled on and accepted an opportunity to work therapeutically with people coming from different parts of former Yugoslavia. They had all found themselves in the UK, misplaced, with no choice in the process. I spent hours meeting them singly, in regular one-to-one encounters. I hoped that, at some point, they could join a group together, so that we could all continue trying to make sense of the civil war and their different experiences of it. But this did not happen at the time. It did not feel possible. The pain felt too raw. The loss, shame, fury and death were too overwhelming and still very much undigested on a wider scale. The chance for reconciliation in such a way needed to wait. I eventually accepted the reality of it.

## Conclusion

Reflecting on these transitional, in-between experiences in life, psychotherapy and psychogeographical drifting, I have been curious about a sense of estrangement in all of them.

Psychoanalyst Gregorio Kohon creatively explores this particular sense in his discussion on the aesthetic experience. He says that, for the aesthetic experience to happen:

> … the subject [the therapist/the drifter] has to be ready
> and willing to undergo some form of depersonalisation, to
> experience some sense of unreality; the subject must risk,
> however briefly, losing the boundaries that keep the self safe and
> sound... If we are going not so much 'to understand' the artistic
> object [the subject of therapy/the geographical, cultural and
> political surrounding] as to allow ourselves, instead, to become

involved with it, there will be a demand for uncertainty to be tolerated: uncertainty, opaqueness, doubt. The relationship with the artistic object cannot be resolved: it is steeped in the ambiguity of something familiar and unfamiliar, uncanny. (Kohon, 2016: 5 &19)

The engagement with the space in between the inner and the outer world seems to me to be a very important part of life. It may be that this raw involvement with the uncertainty of this space can, in fact, make us feel at home, regardless of where in the world we find ourselves, both in peace and during wars.

I wonder if psychotherapy and psychogeography, as well as art in general, may actually be there to assist in investigating these in-between moments in life: the points when we feel at odds with our self and/or with our surroundings, when we may not be sure who we really are and where we are. These are the experiences that we may need to continue to master throughout life and its numerous changes. And the artistry in negotiating these in-between states, I believe, can be truly embraced only in relationship to others.

## References

Adichie CN (2009). *The danger of a single story.* [Video.] TED Global; July. www.ted.com/talks/chimamanda_adichie_the_danger_of_a_single_story?language=e (accessed 15 April 2019).

Adichie CN (2006). *Half of a Yellow Sun.* London: HarperCollins.

Bion WR (1962). The psycho-analytic study of thinking. *International Journal of Psycho-Analysis 43*: 306–310.

Coverley M (2018). *Psychogeography.* Harpenden: Pocket Essentials.

Foulkes SH (1964). *Therapeutic Group Analysis.* London: Allen & Unwin.

Huskinson L (ed) (2016). *The Urban Uncanny: a collection of interdisciplinary studies.* Abingdon: Routledge.

Goldsworthy V (1998). *Inventing Ruritania: the imperialism of the imagination.* New Haven, CT: Yale University Press.

Jaćimović S (1993). *Mirska Pjenija.* Choreographic images for soloists, orchestra and choir. [Video.] www.youtube.com/playlist?list=PLA8E2F99F4626CCEF

Jaćimović S (1990). *What is Going On?* Composed for symphony orchestra. http://srdjany.tripod.com/

Jaćimović S (1987). *La Flamme de l'Orange.* Composed for symphony orchestra. http://srdjany.tripod.com/

Jaćimović V (1999). *Creation, Destruction and Recreation: on finding a balance between external influences on the group and its internal dynamics.* Unpublished theory paper, Institute of Group Analysis.

Jaćimović V (1998). *Mirroring: creating and recreating of the self – a space in between.* Unpublished theory paper, Institute of Group Analysis.

Kohon G (2016). *Reflections on the aesthetic experience: psychoanalysis and the uncanny.* New York, NY: Routledge.

Kristeva J (1991). *Strangers to Ourselves.* New York, NY: Columbia University Press.

Ogden T (1999). *Reverie and Interpretation.* London: Karnac Books.

Roberts J (1993). Intervening to establish and maintain therapeutic environment. In: Kennard D, Roberts J, Winter DA (eds). *A Work Book of Group-Analytic Interventions.* London: Jessica Kingsley (pp92–97).

Royle N (2003). *The Uncanny.* Manchester: Manchester University Press.

Tiernan C (2011). *Immortal Beloved.* London: Hodder & Stoughton.

Winnicott DW (1971). *Playing and Reality.* London: Tavistock Publications.

Yeats WB. The second coming. In: Yeats WB (2000). *The Collected Poems of WB Yeats.* Ware: Wordsworth Editions.

Zinkin L (1983). Malignant mirroring. *Group Analysis 16*(2): 113–126.

# 10 | Mapmaking
## Chris Rose

Winnie the Pooh had a map of the wood; Bilbo Baggins had a map of Middle Earth; the Swallows and Amazons had maps, and so did Harry Potter. I studied all of them, for they were integral to the story. In the years between reading AA Milne and JK Rowling, there were maps I drew myself, found in books, played with in games, and eventually used to find my way around places. Ordnance Survey maps and the *AA Road Atlas* became important possessions, to be followed, but not entirely replaced, by GPS systems, confidently directing the way.

Maps and mapmaking have threaded their way through my life, from Middle Earth to Google Earth, from survey to mind-map, and into the therapy room. This chapter is a personal and idiosyncratic view of that process, meandering across different types of landscape, drawn to some and disturbed by others. It is constrained by culture and history, as we all are. I am white, female, middle class and literate – there are different, perhaps more interesting perspectives that I acknowledge but must leave to others to explore. This is a piece of writing that attempts to engage with reflection and resonance, while suggesting links between the map as external object and internal processes and images. It walks, in the style of psychogeography, through territories, thoughts and ideas that are linked by my own free associative processes, before ending up in the therapy room.

## A brisk sunny walk

I set out on a cheery path, inspired by childhood recollections of exciting books with maps that I needed to regularly check in order to really understand what was happening. Of course, I have a folded paper map in my rucksack that gives me confidence to tackle the unknown. I was taught how to read maps in school geography lessons, and thereafter thought of them as good objects – interesting, enjoyable and, at times, indispensable. Like many others, I had unerring faith in them, believing them truthful and trustworthy. I see the maps now, poking from cagoule pockets or hanging in transparent folders, reliable companions for any walk into new territory.

Our familiar environment is matched by a familiar version of self; they are blended together even if we rarely appreciate this. It is only when we move into places where we are not sure of our footing that our inner securities may become destabilised by the unfamiliarity. It shows, perhaps, in a bubbling excitement, or an underlying unease. Am I the same person, wandering through an unfamiliar French town, pottering at home in the garden, walking along a Northern shore? Yes and no. It is the map that I hold onto, turn to for reassurance in these transitions.

A map cannot offer the tactile comfort or warmth of a teddy bear or a piece of cloth; it is, rather, a cerebral, cognitive version of a security blanket. Its presence enables us to step outside the door, to leave home and explore, to bridge the known and the unknown. Maps may lack the cuddly qualities of a blanket or bear, but people become very attached to them, to these battered, weather-stained companions of many miles and adventures – and, like old bears, they become collectors' items, documenting over time the changing landscapes and cityscapes of our environment, as well as our own particular forays into the wilderness.

Maps, just like other transitional objects, cannot fully protect us from the complexity and unpredictability of life. In this instance, we have to bridge the distance between the two-dimensional systematic diagram and a landscape rich in features that elude accurate measurement: mud, panoramas, noise, stinging nettles, animals, weather, scents, trees, flowers etc. This is what

Thoreau understood and attempted to capture. Better known as a writer, Henry David Thoreau was a trained and well-respected surveyor, commissioned in 1859 to measure and catalogue the bridges across the Concord River in Massachusetts, in a dispute between mill owners and farmers. He immersed himself in the task, at times in the river itself, and produced a map seven and a half feet long, annotated with descriptions of trees, wildlife, swimming holes and historical notes that refused to strip the river of its character (Miller, 2018).

Now, online street maps enable us to switch from two- to three-dimensional images, so that, when stepping out, we are ever more confident that we 'know' where we are going. But still there is the birdsong, the sudden downpour, the litter, the smell of silage or take-away food that cannot be mapped in this way. The security of 'knowing' beforehand is always imperfect. In the end, the journey begins by that step out of the door and daring to physically experience the world.

This is one of the central aspects of psychogeography – physically encountering the environment through walking. Psychogeographers wander at random into unfamiliar places, often the forgotten, derelict, dark corners of the landscape, boldly leaving the map behind and trusting that being lost will only be a transitional state. Perhaps related to the male bias – Morag Rose's 'curse of the *flâneur*' (see Chapter 6) – in early psychogeography, there is confidence that 'lost' will refer to physical location rather than the sense of self; that being lost is fun, an adventure that will have a happy ending, a noble endeavour even. But I wonder if perhaps 'being lost' is too strong a term – maybe 'disorientated' would be more accurate?

In our map-soaked culture, it is difficult not to have some sort of internalised map, a way of understanding location and navigation. We might have a rough or approximate idea of where we are, even though the particular street is unknown. We might be confident too in our ability to retrace our steps, marking turns and landmarks in our mind so that, like Hansel and Gretel, we have a trail of stones or breadcrumbs to guide us back to the known. Or, most likely nowadays, we have a mobile phone with GPS navigation.

Perhaps, though, there remains some internalised map, a visual image of a screen or paper map or other awareness of location derived from a 'sense of direction'. This sense has, for most of us, become a vestigial link with a way-finding skill that was once commonplace, now so diminished that we need to be taught again how to use the navigational clues around us: sun, moon, stars, weather, land, sea, animals, plants (Huth, 2013).

## Another type of map

For those of us brought up in a culture where the map is an object, a visual representation of geographical territory, it is hard to imagine the complexity and richness of cultures where space is integrated with time and movement and navigation is a subheading in a narrative.

The most well-known example is probably the 'songlines' created by the native peoples of Australia, which hold a powerful fascination for Westerners – perhaps because they resonate with some long-lost aspect of our own history. The way-finding abilities are legendary, but the functional navigational skills are deeply entwined with cultural, spiritual beliefs and practices, making it impossible to extract them.

There are other examples where cultural practices and pathways are integrated, such as the Bushmen of Namibia. Their geographical knowledge is essentially social. Navigating involves going somewhere to meet someone to do something, and the geography is a part of the social discourse, rather than having some separate existence in its own right. In a similar way, the Inuit of the Canadian Arctic maintain a network of trails that disappear as the snow melts and are reinstated as the snow falls again, without any maps. As with the Bushmen, travel for the Inuit is about going somewhere in order to find something and meet someone. The trails are places of social interaction where information and news are shared across the dispersed community, and some have been reinstated after the snowfall for at least two centuries (Heft, 2013).

For me, these are important because they show clearly how moral rules, physical sensation, personal and social relationships, cultural practices and spiritual beliefs are co-constructed into maps that show how to navigate through life. The contemporary drawn, printed or digital map may appear to have been drained of all such significance, presenting an uncontroversial and impartial visual guide to movement from A to B, but I suggest this is not so. Embedded within these supposedly neutral artefacts lie cultural narratives of social and spiritual organisation, dominance, possession, conflict, disputes, fantasy and imagination.

We are raised as children within a network of beliefs and relationships that structure our being. The ability to question these ways of life comes later, when we begin to understand that there are other versions of parents, siblings, language, gods, food and ways of life. Then comes the question, 'Whose rules are we following?'

## Whose map is it anyway?

Although I started this chapter with a very individual statement of my relationship with maps, there is of course a bigger picture. The Western cultural definition of the self as an independent and autonomous individual obscures the extent to which we are not only shaped but co-constructed by the social and cultural environment that spawns us. It may seem clear that, in older societies, the group – community, tribe, clan, congregation – was the major formative influence, and that the webs of relationship defined a person far more than individual attributes, which were themselves seen as aspects of the collective. Having successfully destroyed many of these communities in the pursuit of profit and control, we struggle to push against the contemporary propaganda to recognise our own web of interconnectedness.

My interest in maps, for example, was not merely a product of my reading skills; nor was it some family fascination that I inherited. I was raised in a society that was drenched in maps, where the conventional ways of conceptualising spatial configurations had become so much part of unconscious mental processes that it was hidden from view.

Centuries of linear perspective have convinced us Europeans that this is the only accurate way to portray the environment. Our ideas of reality have been so shaped by how we conventionally represent it that, when an artist breaks free from this way of seeing, we label the work as 'abstract'.

Early maps depicted the world in a very different way. Important places were bigger, towns were viewed from multiple aspects, things were placed in symbolic relationship to each other, pictures conveyed a feeling tone; the viewer was invited to experience the map as if travelling within it rather than looking at it as a single view. The most significant place politically or spiritually sat in the central position: Babylon in ancient Mesopotamia; Delphi in Greece; Mecca and Jerusalem in Islamic and Christian countries. Each culture was mapped as if it were the centre of the world, its navel, and this 'omphalos syndrome' is still visible today.

Some maps may have functioned as a travel guide but, mostly, physical navigation was not their purpose. For example, the famous Ebsdorf map of 1250 that places Jerusalem at its heart was concerned with enlightenment, not travel. The map was essential in the search for meaning, for the right pathway to travel through life without ever leaving home.

The pathway that I am following right now branches ahead of me. On the right, the signpost reads 'imagination', pointing to a narrow and mysterious way ahead. To the left there is a broad and well-surfaced track signposted to 'power'. I have a feeling that they will link up at some point, so I take the left fork. Very quickly, the path turns uphill, rocky and strenuous.

## Land grabs: where the path gets darker

There was little if any distinction between mapmaking and art until the early 15th century, when linear perspective was developed, and subsequently accepted as the best, most accurate way of representing space in a two-dimensional format. Mapmaking became surveying and measuring – a precise, scientific discipline accepted for its accuracy in representing the world in two dimensions. Driven by the need to provide detailed knowledge of territories and possessions, it enabled the colonial land grab of what was labelled the 'new world' and continues to be an essential tool in struggles to control and dominate the landscape.

The map is the ally of wealthy elites who, by drawing boundaries, are asserting ownership. Each empire needs to proclaim its extensiveness, advertise its reach and dominion. People are displaced or incorporated by those who have the means – guns, money and mendacity – to claim ownership of land. Common land is under constant threat, its history full of desperate tales of enclosures and clearances. Communities are displaced by developers, populations are displaced by government fiat, walls are built, and sometimes demolished; the history of making maps is one of conflict, exploitation and appropriation. Many of the contemporary world conflicts can be traced back to arbitrary boundaries drawn across territories by those who had power and weapons but cared nothing for the inhabitants or ecology of the land.

Land is at the heart of power and security. Our relationship with land is fundamental, literally the ground upon which we have our being, but as the waves of refugees and migrants show, it is so easily torn apart.

> 'Knowing one's place' has become a derogatory comment about class hierarchy, but the local is where people live their history and geography and both are infused with emotional attachment and personal identity. (Bunting, 2016: 250)

Madeleine Bunting's accounts of the Outer Hebrides emphasise the significance of the Gaelic language to express attachment to land: *'dúthchas* expresses the collective right to the land of those who use it, and *còraichean* expresses the idea of people belonging to the land' (Bunting, 2016: 249).

Collective rights to land challenge the ideology of capitalism, which sees land as potential profit, and mapmaking has often been the ally of those wishing to exploit the land for commercial and political purposes. When submitting plans for a super-quarry on the island of Harris, the company involved presented maps that replaced the names of places with numbers, thereby erasing their history and relationship to the inhabitants. This is a 20th century example of the process whereby the mapping of many indigenous territories around the world emptied them of inhabitants and histories in the rapacious desire for ownership of natural resources. By representing the land as wilderness, for example, it becomes open for appropriation.

What is omitted in mapmaking is as crucial as what is included. Motorway service stations, shopping malls, golf courses, retail outlets, historic monuments, synagogues, hostels and night shelters, mosques, food banks, rubbish tips, recycling facilities, cycle paths, disabled access toilets, free parking, playgrounds, skate parks, bridle paths, caravans, refugee shelters, gated communities, empty shops, wildlife reserves, unsurfaced roads, unlit alleyways, litter bins, high rise blocks, and on and on. There are choices to be made about what goes in and what is left out, even in a system such as 'open mapping', where those interested can upload details to an open access online map… but interested in what? Whose map is it anyway?

> Both in the selectivity of their content and in their signs and styles of representation, maps are a way of conceiving, articulating and structuring the human world which is biased towards, promoted by, and exerts an influence upon particular sets of social relations. By accepting such premises it becomes easier to see how appropriate they are to manipulation by the powerful in society. (Harley, 2008)

## Boundaries

I have come to a brick wall topped with barbed wire. There is only one small, concrete pathway around the wall where it is possible to walk, and I can see nothing but the line of concrete, walls both sides, and the sky above.

Lines drawn on maps may look benign but in reality can be brutal. The static, visual representation, the line that separates one territory from the next, proclaims this is how it is. Before long, it implies that this is how it is meant to be or has always been. The map becomes the authoritative source of information, defining who has crossed the line – an intruder, a trespasser, a poacher, a spy, a revolutionary.

We need boundaries, just as we need maps. There is too much complexity and we must simplify, abstract, in order to comprehend and make a life. Boundaries keep us safe: the curtain walls in our minds, defended with cannons or boiling oil. Inside the castle, people like me; outside, the others; infidels, homosexuals, blacks, 'abnormals', aliens, whatever and whoever threatens our internal assurances of being at least all right, if not righteous. A cultural language of possession, entitlement, acquisition and progress determines where we place the boundaries and we rarely question whose interests they serve, assuming that, of course, they protect us or are self-evidently 'right'. Therapy can be a revolutionary process, sneaking through guarded passages or climbing previously impregnable walls to reveal the paradoxical nature of boundaries themselves. Boundaries offer to keep us safe by keeping us locked away.

Suddenly the path is joined by a small meandering track that looks familiar. I'm ready for a different sort of landscape and, in this interesting but uncomfortable territory between security and entrapment, my imagination is ready to lift off. I'm thinking about the place that captures these two elements perfectly – the island.

## Islands of imagination

The island has a powerful appeal. Its obvious geographical limits offer containment, within which to play out fantasies and desires. Romanticised as a location for self-understanding and contemplation, a sanctuary from urbanised, industrialised society where it is possible to reconnect with the natural environment, the island has had many propagandists. *Treasure Island*, *Peter Pan*, *Swallows and Amazons*, Tracey Island (*Thunderbirds*), Kirrin Island (the *Famous Five* series) – there are so many works of fiction that rely on the particular characteristics of an isolated and contained land mass surrounded by water.

In children's fiction, the physical boundary is often accompanied by freedom from the constraints of parental control. In adult fiction, there can be a related liberation from norms and obligations, where we can encounter in ourselves our 'true' nature, our fantasy of who we might be without the restrictions of social living. It gives expression to our conflicted desire to be rid of 'the other' while (usually) being forced into intense relationship with the particular others who are also on the island.

The island may free us from constraints, a vision of self-indulgence, while paradoxically being a place where habits and values have to be re-established in order to live in 'wild' environments. Robinson Crusoe, in Defoe's eponymous novel (1719/2007), 'tamed' the island. He farmed and fished and built, through constant hard work, while always reading his bible and praying… and, as in all empire-building narratives, he dominated the native and made him a willing servant. He was the model for the determined, hard-working, God-fearing male who could, through effort and will, create his own earthly kingdom.

William Golding, in *Lord of the Flies* (1954), reveals another far darker outcome. Orwell's bleak and prophetic *Nineteen Eighty-Four* (1949) was written on the island of Jura, in the Hebrides. There, distant from the horrors of both war and society, he lived a physically demanding but rewarding life in rural isolation, from which vantage point he was able to contemplate and create his vision of future horrors.

There is always a dark side of the island. Remoteness is both sanctuary and torment. Containment is both security and entrapment. Those seduced by the positives are often defeated by the negatives, as demonstrated by the abandoned grand houses and gardens of the super-rich in the Hebrides.

But as a metaphor for the self, these contradictions offer a rich site for exploration. There are two main approaches: for those who see the self as a unitary organism, the search becomes a treasure hunt for our perceived notion of what lies at the heart of our being. We may have to travel through perilous terrain in order to find whatever it is – a spirit, a soul, a God, a true self, the meaning of life. The island is only one possible location for this search. John Bunyan, in *The Pilgrim's Progress* (1678/2003), constructed the journey as the search for the true relationship with God, and he led his main protagonist, Christian, through many landscapes reminiscent of the Bedfordshire geography that he himself was familiar with. We are wired into landscape, finding in it the ways to tell our stories and search out our desires.

For those who think of the self as a multiple organisation, the varieties of landscape give scope to explore its different aspects or configurations. In this approach, the dark and challenging areas are not travelled through and surmounted but are always present, as are the sandy beaches and breath-taking views.

An island map can dispense with any line between cartography and art or between seriousness and playfulness. Try it out – draw your own island. It is a playful but revealing exercise with scope for many different habitats where the various aspects of ourselves can find room for expression. It might be called navel gazing, another version of the omphalos syndrome, but the imagination and playfulness involved gives it a far wider view than that other self-centred map we are now so familiar with.

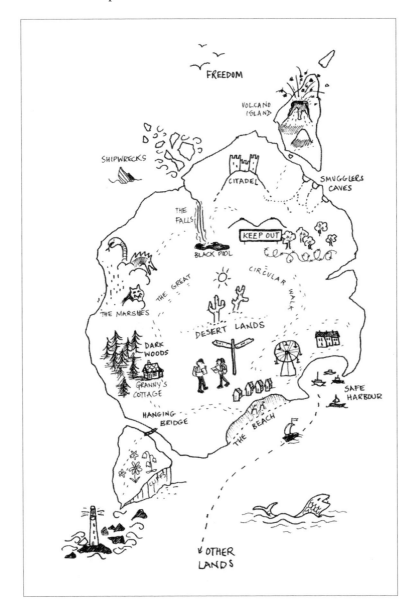

## Where am I?

Abruptly, the path opens out into a tarmac road, leading me to the outskirts of a place I half recognise. Now I need to check my bearings.

When I unfold a paper map, searching for directions, I have to locate myself within its expanse. The landscape dominates and I gradually search out my own location. When I open Google maps on my smartphone, the opposite happens: my location springs out, the blue circle within a fragment of context. Here the world centres on Me, revealing itself only as I progress through it, screen by screen. The bigger picture is fragmented and obscured.

Fading out the geographical context means losing touch with our environment, so evident in the crisis of climate change. Despite its capacity to revolutionise our views of the world, this is a technology perfectly suited to the narrow vision of the individual. We can see amazing images of the earth from space, but is our first response to search for ourselves, our country, town, street, house?

Place is bound together with history, and the myopic focus on here and now, without consideration of what was here before and the meanings embedded in it, impoverishes our understanding and experience. There are parallels here with the fading out of history.

> History's expertise, and most dangerously its perspective, are being lost in our inability to look beyond the here and now. We stumble into crises of finance and inequality with ignorance of economic history, and forget even the recent background to our current policies. We fail to think in the long term and miss a growing environmental catastrophe. We refuse help to millions of refugees by turning away from our own history. As technology and globalisation bring the world closer together, we have narrowed rather than broadened our perspective. (Kissane, 2017)

Christopher Kissane's warnings about dismissing the historical perspective resonate powerfully with the failure to grasp the importance of place, of our geography. Psychotherapy gets caught in the same impetus, focusing on the individual, drained of relational, historical, economic, political, cultural and geographical context. The message that the individual is in charge of their destiny has a powerful hold in contemporary Western society, but lived reality tells us we are shaped and created through the relational, cultural, historical, sociopolitical context of our lives. This is not the backdrop – it is the fabric from which we are woven. Changing attitudes, thoughts and behaviours can be a highly successful therapeutic approach, but we cannot wrench ourselves from our context – and that is, for many, the reason why therapy needs a broader vision and a longer time scale.

Of course! That's where I have reached – the landscape of psychotherapy.

## Internal landscapes

> It is completely dark and cold. I can't hear a sound apart from my own breathing. I am crouched down against a wall and when I feel behind me all I find is cold, damp brickwork. I stand up and feel that the bricks go on above my head – for miles, I imagine. Inside, I am screaming and sobbing and gasping, but here in the dark I am silent with despair. There seems to be no way out of this place.

This is one of the many landscapes of depression. Being able to express emotion through descriptions of place can form a starting point in allowing another person access to the bleakness. As a psychotherapist, I see this as the place where the client and I begin, from which we may be able to move, and to which we will undoubtedly return at times. We set off from a tightly enclosed, entrapping space, where the landscape has in effect collapsed into a mineshaft, a pit, a rabbit hole, a chasm – there are many ways of describing this emotional/geographical feature. Our conversations can hopefully weave themselves into a rope ladder that can be used to climb out of the pit, into a different sort of landscape.

We may end up in another familiar place: a boundless, featureless plain, strewn with rocks but without vegetation, where the land and the sky are grey and motionless. The view is the same in every direction. There are no landmarks or clues as to which direction to move in, and there is no motivation to search. We sit together and gaze at the greyness, feel the deadness in the air and the hopelessness wash over us. All that effort to get out of the pit, and now we are here in a grey nothingness. It is a landscape that has been drained of life, where nothing grows or moves. I am searching for a map – something inside myself that I can bring to the landscape that will facilitate a change: a bird in the sky, a cloud, a lizard – any form of life. Who knows what is over the horizon, and I need to hold out hope that this grey deadness is not all there is.

Perhaps, if we look more closely, we can see that the grey is not uniform, but rather has subtle shades of lighter and darker, more yellowish or bluish…Together, we may move towards one of these patches and stumble across a patch of sparse grass, a place where at least something can grow. Maybe it is a dried-up river bed? Perhaps, if we follow it, we might come across more vegetation – maybe a stunted shrub? The landscape is beginning to have features now that we are able to look more closely at it.

I expect at some point we will come across a swamp. It usually arrives after the tough journey out of the featureless plain, when we are beginning to think perhaps it is possible to navigate this landscape after all. There are tracks in the long grass, perhaps made by animals, as we certainly have not reached the land of people yet. Suddenly my client stumbles as their foot sinks into deep slime, pulling them over and down into the viscous mud. I find a plank and we struggle to regain firm land.

Now we need a much more detailed map. We need to mark and recognise where the land changes colour or the vegetation shifts slightly, until we can find a route that goes around these danger points. At this stage, the mapmaking becomes more sophisticated, with symbols of danger and caution and contours for high and low-lying land. My client takes the map with them and when they return for our next conversation I can enquire about its usefulness. Have there been any more swamp episodes? How did they get out? Have they discovered a better route? Are there more warning signs to add to the map?

Internal landscapes do not alter in any linear, time-regulated fashion. In any day we can find ourselves in any number of disparate places. I am not describing here the smooth path of therapeutic progress but picking out some characteristic places in order to think about the process whereby we navigate life. We need our own maps, and a therapeutic relationship can offer the opportunity to draw up new ones or modify existing ones. As a psychotherapist, I have the luxury of experiencing a lot of other people's maps, and these give me a familiarity with landscapes that are not my own. Many of them resonate with mine, but some lie outside my parameters, helping me in turn expand my own map and refine my mapmaking abilities.

For many clients, the map is the problem. They are travelling up and down, forwards and backwards across a tightly defined and very familiar set of streets and landmarks. There are major avenues: 'I'm too much for people', 'If I start crying, I would never stop', 'Keep your distance', 'Relationships never work', 'I'm a terrible person', 'Why do people always leave me?' There are lots of well-trodden streets, such as 'Nobody really cares', 'Everyone takes and no one gives me anything', 'I'm only trying to help', 'It's not my problem' or 'It's all my fault'. We are cycling or walking around an estate, visiting every street in turn, spending hours in the rather run-down and desolate playground or scrap of parkland, before turning back once more to walk the same old streets.

We need a new map with bigger horizons and new perspectives, and sometimes the old map just needs to be folded up and put away. The more we insist that somewhere in its streets we will find 'the answer' or the 'solution', the more we deceive ourselves. Under the guise of working hard, we can remain in this uncomfortable – yet profoundly comfortable – impasse forever. The map has become the attachment object and weaning the client onto a more complex and more open version can be a difficult task for all concerned. The task of therapy is always to expand the map, for both client and therapist.

We may find our way out of the estate and onto the open road, but the exhilaration may be short lived. Instead of walking through the streets we know by heart, we can end up driving up and down the motorway network. Motorway driving is fuelled by high emotion and the absence of reflection. We know the route and set off, gathering speed as we go. Here's an example.

Every time Sarah spends the night at her sister's, her partner Mike knows she is planning to leave him. His body reacts with panic symptoms and his emotions swing wildly between anger, self-pity, sadness and guilt – so rapidly that it is impossible to identify anything clearly except a globalised distress. He acts this out in a ritual of binge drinking, watching porn videos and repeated attempts to call Sarah… all of which encourage Sarah to stay away from him.

Mike is on his own motorway, driving at speed, in his one fixed response to a situation and always covering the same territory, until it becomes taken for granted that there can be no other way of reacting. Thoughtless motorway driving can end badly.

Motorways may be very efficient for certain sorts of travel in some situations, but they are bland, monotonous and pay little regard to the subtleties of the landscape they cut through. Finding other routes, smaller and more interesting roads that open up different views, could help Mike to look around and escape his distress routine. This is, hopefully, what therapy can offer.

For many clients, maps provide helpful metaphors – perhaps because they can provide both a cognitive, 'practical' way of understanding their situation and an imaginative possibility. The map, like the teddy bear, is real in the sense that it is a tangible object. Its role as a guide to navigation is clear, but, like the bear, it encompasses other layers of function and possibility, straddling the boundaries of 'common sense' and 'hidden meanings'.

In most long-term therapy, there is a point where the client tells me that I must be bored, listening to the same old things repeating week after week. 'Going round in circles' is another travelling metaphor that can be opened out, with the help of a map, into something less despondent and negative. It needs the sort of map that Thoreau drew, paying attention to the details, for these are the signs of change and life in what otherwise appears to be a repetitive trudge along a well-worn track. Those internalised routes through life that have eventually brought people into therapy are powerful and persistent. Despite our best conscious efforts, we are seemingly glued to them, tenaciously attached. Lasting changes come about through incremental shifts; recognising that this week's walk has pushed further into the undergrowth, stopping to admire the bluebells, noticing a small track leading uphill, taking the path around the bramble patch rather than insisting on walking through it.

Mapmaking always involves abstraction. It protects us from being overwhelmed by the complexity of life and is a necessary, valuable process. But there are points where its simplicity or rigidity is suffocating, and in order to breathe we have to look again, more closely and creatively.

## 'You have reached your destination'

A map can take many forms: a physical object, an artwork, a precise calculation, a technological achievement, a way of thinking. They can be put to many uses: as tools in diverse struggles and conflicting desires, pathways to exploration and imagination, trusted companions and mendacious opponents. It is this capacity to hold together so many paradoxes that makes them resilient and fascinating.

Once upon a time, I took for granted the possibility of scientific rational objectivity. The map was unbiased, accurate and completely reliable. Once upon a time, I entertained the idea that it was possible to be an objective, unbiased therapist – the blank screen upon which the other's life could be projected. Both of these beliefs rested on the possibility of severing science from imagination and individual from individual. Those assumptions are long gone; our desire to divide and compartmentalise is undone by the irrepressible, bubbling emergence of chaos and the complexity of human relationships.

## References

Bunting M (2016). *Love of Country: a Hebridean journey*. London: Granta.

Bunyan J (1678/2003). *The Pilgrim's Progress* (WR Owens, ed). Oxford: Oxford University Press.

Defoe D (1719/2007). *Robinson Crusoe* (T Keymer, ed). Oxford: Oxford University Press.

Golding W (1954). *Lord of the Flies*. London: Faber & Faber.

Harley JB (2008). Maps, knowledge and power. In: Henderson G, Waterstone M (eds). *Geographic Thought: a praxis perspective*. Abingdon: Routledge.

Heft H (2013). Environment, cognition and culture: reconsidering the cognitive map. *Journal of Environmental Psychology 33*(2013): 14–25.

Huth JE (2013). *The Lost Art of Finding our Way*. Cambridge, MA: Harvard University Press.

Kissane C (2017). Historical myopia is to blame for the attacks on Mary Beard. [Online.] *The Guardian*; 11 August. www.theguardian.com/books/2017/aug/11/reformation-2017-christopher-kissane-history (accessed 14 April 2019).

Miller D (2018). A map of radical bewilderment: on the liberation cartography of Henry David Thoreau. [Online.] *Places Journal;* March. https://doi.org/10.22269/180306 (accessed 18 May 2018).

Orwell G (1949). *Nineteen Eighty-Four*. London: Secker & Warburg.

# Contributors

## Authors

**Liz Bondi** divides her time between her counselling/psychotherapy practice and the University of Edinburgh, where she contributes to postgraduate counsellor training and doctoral supervision. Liz began her academic career in human geography (and is Professor of Social Geography), which she continued while training part-time in counselling in the 1990s, before making a sideways move into what is now Counselling, Psychotherapy and Applied Social Sciences at the University of Edinburgh. She is founding editor of the journal *Emotion, Space and Society* and author of numerous academic papers as well as co-editor or co-author of several books.

**Benedict Hoff** completed his PhD in cultural geography/queer studies at Liverpool University in 2012. He is Clinical Lead for Mental Health at the London-based sexual health charity Spectra, where he works as an integrative counsellor and leads a Public Health England-funded mindfulness-based chemsex recovery programme for gay and bisexual men. He is an associate mindfulness teacher with Breathworks, supporting people living with stress, chronic pain and long-term health conditions. He has a long-standing interest in cinema, cities and urban subcultures and is author of *Reprojecting The City: dissident sexualities in recent Latin American cinema* (2017).

**Karen Izod** is a consultant to organisational change, a researcher and writer working from a relational systems-psychodynamic perspective. She is joint author of *Resource-ful Consulting* (2014) and joint editor of *Mind-ful Consulting* (2009). Recent publications explore the nature of attachment to place, and her poetry concerns wild places, city spaces, people, politics, remembering and forgetting. Karen is Visiting Research Fellow at the University of West of England and Professional Partner at the Tavistock Institute. She was Poet in Residence at the Association for Psychosocial Studies Conference 2018. www.karenizod.com

**Valentina Krajnović** (née **Jaćimović**) is a group analyst, teacher, supervisor and a training course convenor. She is a member of the Institute of Group Analysis and the Council for Psychoanalysis and Jungian Analysis, and is accredited by the UKCP. She initially trained as a clinical psychologist in Belgrade, Serbia, and has since worked therapeutically and in a supervisory role with both individuals and groups, in organisational settings and in private practice. Her special interest is in promoting communication among people and in the possibility of a dialogue repairing the damage done within the individual microcosms as well as the macrocosm of a wider society and different cultures.

**Diane Parker** is a coach, group facilitator and dance movement psychotherapist currently working in forensic and community mental health. In addition to leading women's groups, she also works with men in prison as a life coach and psychotherapist. She is a contributor to the *Forensic Arts Therapies Anthology of Practice and Research* (2016), and she has contributed to a number of journals, including BACP's *Therapy Today*.

**Richard Phillips** is Professor of Human Geography at the University of Sheffield. His research and teaching explore curiosity, adventure, encounter, creative research methods and fieldwork. Richard's publications include *Fieldwork for Human Geography* (2012), *Mapping Men and Empire: a geography of adventure* (1996), and *Sex, Politics and Empire* (2006). His interest in exploring and becoming mindfully attentive to ordinary places – the subject of his chapter in this book – is developed in a collection of essays on Georges Perec's geographies, which will be published in 2019.

**Chris Powell** is a group analyst, supervisor and organisational consultant, formerly Head of Psychological Therapies at the Retreat in York. He now works independently, using group analytic approaches outside clinical settings and founded Café Psychologique – open group discussions from a psychological perspective that now take place in Prague and Sydney as well as around the UK. He also continues to run the Room To Breathe group, meeting once every season to walk and talk in the open air in the Yorkshire Dales. www.spark.uk.net

**Chris Rose** is a group psychotherapist, supervisor and consultant working in private practice and higher education. She has extensive experience in counselling and psychotherapy training and has written *The Personal Development Group: the student's guide* (2008) and is the editor of *Self Awareness and Personal Development: resources for psychotherapists and counsellors* (2011). She is also an urban sketcher and printmaker.

**Morag Rose** is an *anarchoflâneuse* and walking artist-activist-academic. In 2006 she co-founded the Loiterers Resistance Movement (LRM), a Manchester-based collective interested in psychogeography, public space, creative walking and uncovering hidden stories and power structures. Morag worked in community development and voluntary sector support before her PhD in Urban Studies and Planning at the University of Sheffield. She is a now a Lecturer in Geography at the University of Liverpool. Morag has presented, performed and exhibited internationally and the LRM continues to meet on the first Sunday of every month. All are welcome to join for a wander and wonder.

**Jane Samuels** is a Mancunian artist and educator. She completed her degree and Master's in Fine Art at Salford University, and is a walking-artist and psychogeographer with a particular interest in the politics of place, both in natural and built environments. She has curated and exhibited in the UK and internationally, served as a photography judge for the 2018 ADC (Art Directors Club) awards in New York and can eat her body weight in pizza. Samuels is politically active, most recently in direct action against the UK badger cull, and the principles and politics of equity underpin her writing, visual art and teaching. She lives and works from her studio in the Pennine hills.

**Phil Wood** is an independent writer, researcher and activist in urban policy and culture based in Yorkshire. He was in local government for 18 years and since 2000 has worked around the world as a consultant on managing change. He is principal advisor to the Council of Europe on its Intercultural Cities programme, based on his book *The Intercultural City: planning for diversity advantage* (2008). He is the co-founder of the 4th World Congress of Psychogeography. Phil holds a MA with distinction in European Cultural Planning from De Montfort University.

## Illustrators

**Rob Foster** is a wood turner and artist, who joined the Birmingham Urban Sketchers group hoping to improve his drawing abilities and meet a partner. Instead he found friends, support and self-confidence. He writes: 'There will not exist a time when I don't venture out to draw and paint outdoors, even if I am the last man standing.'

**Ed Harker** is a nursery/kindergarten teacher by training and is now the head-teacher of an infant school in Bath, UK. He started drawing from life every day seven years ago and has been sharing his sketching progress since 2012 through a blog at mostlydrawing.com

**Caroline Parkinson** is a West Midlands-based illustrator, a budget traveller and a compulsive sketcher who graduated from Loughborough University with a BA in Illustration in 2004. Since then her work has been used in animation, comics, television, education and podcasts. She is currently working on a 200-page graphic novel about 11th century Japan and bakes a mean Victoria sponge.

**Simone Ridyard** is an architect and senior lecturer in Interior Design at Manchester Metropolitan University. She has been involved with urban sketching – participating, teaching, organising and encouraging others – since 2011, and is the author of *Archisketcher: a guide to spotting and sketching urban landscapes* (2015).

# Name index

# Subject index